A Guide to

THE NORTON READER

SEVENTH EDITION

by

Robert E. Hosmer, Jr.
Mount Holyoke College

W. W. NORTON & COMPANY
New York London

Published simultaneously in Canada by Penguin Books Canada Ltd.,
2801 John Street, Markham, Ontario L3R 1B4.

Printed in the United States of America.

First Edition

Library of Congress Cataloging-in-Publication Data

Hosmer, Robert E.
A guide to the Norton reader

p. cm.
"Based on An analytical guide for study, discussion, and writing to the complete and shorter editions of the Norton reader, revised, by Josephine and Earl Schulze" –P.
Rev. ed. of: A guide to the Norton reader, sixth edition / by Craig Bradford Snow, Wayne E. Blankenship. ©1984.
Includes indexes.
ISBN 0-393-95646-6
1. Norton reader. 2. English essays–Study and teaching. 3. American essays–Study and teaching. 4. English language–Rhetoric–Study and teaching. I. Schulze, Josephine. Analytical guide for study, discussion, and writing to the complete and shorter editions of the Norton reader, rev. II. Snow, Craig Bradford. Guide to the Norton reader, sixth edition. III. Norton reader. IV. Title.
PE1122.N683H67 1988
808'.0427–dc 19 87-21885

W. W. Norton & Company, Inc., 500 Fifth Avenue, New York, N.Y. 10110
W. W. Norton & Company Ltd., 37 Great Russell Street, London WC1B 3NU

1 2 3 4 5 6 7 8 9 0

Contents

ETHICS

HISTORY

POLITICS AND GOVERNMENT

SCIENCE

LITERATURE AND THE ARTS

PHILOSOPHY AND RELIGION

Index of Rhetorical Modes and Strategies

Rhetorical Modes

NARRATIVE

DESCRIPTION

EXPOSITION

Essays That Compare and Contrast

Essays That Classify and Divide

Essays That Define

Essays That Analyze a Process

Essays That Analyze Cause/Effect

PERSUASION/ARGUMENT

Rhetorical Strategies

TITLE, AND OPENING AND CLOSING PARAGRAPHS

THESIS, DEVELOPMENT, AND SUPPORT

ORGANIZATION

PERSONA

Preface

This *Guide* has been prepared to offer assistance in use of *The Norton Reader.* It includes suggestions for ways of teaching the essays by means of reading, discussion, and writing. The commentaries, considerations, and questions represent one set of responses–my own–to the rich collection of materials assembled in the Seventh Edition of the *Reader.* In the formulating of the entries for the *Guide*, foremost in my mind have been the needs of the graduate teaching assistant or beginning teacher; I have tried to offer the instructor a clear and solid base on which to build classroom teaching. I have tried to suggest the possibilities of each selection, leaving decisions about approaches and interpretations to the instructor.

The *Guide* follows the contents of *The Norton Reader*, Seventh Edition Shorter, and provides critical material for every selection in that edition; it can, of course, be used with the Regular Edition as well. The Index of Rhetorical Modes and Strategies (pp. xi-xv) cites page references for both versions (NR = Regular Edition, SE = Shorter Edition). The rhetorical index lists all 124 essays in the Shorter Edition and is intended to give guidance to instructors who prefer to organize their courses by rhetorical modes. Following this index are "Notes on Reading and Writing" (p. xxi), reprinted from *The Norton Reader* for convenience. These brief comments are intended to offer students practical advice on reading essays, distilling ideas, and preparing to write. Instructors might assign "Notes" as introductory reading. A number of the *Guide* entries refer to particular discussions in the "Notes."

Each *Guide* entry is meant to serve as a springboard for questions and observations, the instructor's and the student's. Entries consist of three or, in some cases, four parts:

1. A brief introduction to the essay and the author serves as an overview of the selection. This may be supplemented with the biographical sketch of the author in the Appendix of the *Reader.*

2. The part headed "Analytical Considerations" takes up matters of content and rhetoric. This section often begins with four or five objective questions which can serve as a quick review of specifics of the text. This technique will often lead to better discussions.

3. The section on "Comparative Considerations" helps raise the possibilities of comparison among multiple selections by one gifted essayist. The Seventh Edition includes at least four selections by E. B. White, Virginia Woolf, Joan Didion, and Lewis Thomas. *Guide* entries for most of their essays include comparative materials.

4. The section headed "Suggested Writing Assignments," gives three or four suggestions for each essay and draws on key excerpts from the work, other essays related in theme or style, topics that touch students' lives, enduring issues central to liberal education—all with the aim of giving students provocative, wide-ranging ideas for writing.

In its Seventh Edition, *The Norton Reader* continues to provide a consistently challenging and stimulating collection of essays. Many essays will be familiar, retained because instructors have found them compelling and teachable; many essays are new to this edition, selected for the quality of writing and of ideas that they offer. We hope that this *Guide* will help teachers and students explore all that is potential within *The Norton Reader.*

Preparation of this *Guide* has been a complex, absorbing, and finally a rewarding task. In some discussions I have used materials from the previous edition of the *Guide.* For this, credit is gratefully given to Craig Bradford Snow and Wayne E. Blankenship, of the University of Arizona. Many ideas came from my students and colleagues. I have been sustained in my work by a number of people whom I wish to acknowledge here: Joseph J. Ellis, dean of faculty at Mount Holyoke College, and my colleagues in the Department of English: James E. Ellis, chair; Anthony E. Farnham; Richard A. Johnson; and Mary W. McHenry. My debt to Thomas L. Ashton and Charles Kay Smith, University of Massachusetts at Amherst, Sister Jane F. Morrissey, SSJ, Elms College, and Brett Averitt, Westfield State College, master teachers all, cannot be adequately repaid.

I also wish to thank Hubert M. English, Jr., who graciously commented on and helped shape the "Notes on Reading and Writing." Among those at Norton, I wish to thank Joseph B. Janson, who first introduced me to Norton, and Julia A. Reidhead, editor of the Seventh Edition, whose patience and help were willingly given and received.

Robert E. Hosmer, Jr.

Notes on Reading and Writing

> Despair is no good–for the writer, for anyone. Only hope can carry us aloft, can keep us afloat. Only hope, and a certain faith that the incredible structure that has been fashioned by this most strange and ingenious of all mammals cannot end in ruin and disaster. This faith is a writer's faith, for writing itself is an act of faith, nothing else.
>
> –E. B. White, "The Faith of a Writer"

E. B. White's eloquent remarks, delivered on his receiving the National Medal for Literature in 1971, encourage all of us engaged in writing. His words provide a point of departure as we consider the whole project of reading and writing, and the role that *The Norton Reader* can play in enabling you to become a better writer. A *better* writer, for you can already write. That is not just to say that you know the language and some of the "mechanics," like exclamation points, periods, and paragraph indentions, needed to put your thoughts on paper. It also means that you know how to communicate your thoughts in writing, at least some of the time. Sometimes you know what you want to say, other times you do not; sometimes you can find the words to say exactly what you want to, other times you cannot; sometimes you are satisfied with what you have written, other times you are not. If you feel that these last remarks apply to you, do not despair–you are in the company of almost every writer, amateur and professional.

One of the first things to remember about writing derives from an awareness of what human beings are: limited, capable of mistakes, and constantly seeking to understand and express themselves. To recognize that is not to give way to despair; rather, it is to recognize two positive implications for you as a writer. First, your writing cannot be "perfect," and no one is asking you to write the perfect essay. Work toward producing the best piece of writing you can deliver today, but do not be crippled by unrealistic expectations, your own or your instructor's. Second, because you are unique and your experiences and objectives are solely your own, you always have something to add to a text you have read, whether in thought, discussion, or writing.

Recognizing that should give you confidence. Writing, like so many other human activities, goes hand in hand with self-confidence: if you think you can do it, you are halfway there. "Writing itself is an act of faith," primarily in yourself and your abilities, secondarily in language. If you remember how you learned to do certain things–prepare a meal, play a sport, pass an exam–you recall just how important self-confidence is. Of course, preparation and practice are equally important elements in any process. In the process of learning to write better, your preparation–reading, thinking, discussing–and your practice–writing, revising, editing–are essential. In addition, the work of your instructor and your classmates will be invaluable for you. They, too, are writers confronting the same problems that you confront.

The Norton Reader has been designed to play a significant part in that process. It offers a selection of well-written, thought-provoking essays for you to read, reflect on, discuss, and write about. These essays are here for you. The meaning of each essay does not reside "there" on the page, in the essay; nor does it reside solely in you. Furthermore, the essay does not mean whatever you want it to mean. Rather, meaning will emerge from the text and your response to it in that intervening distance between you and the printed page. The meaning that you derive will be tested, modified, rejected, or enhanced when you discuss your ideas in class and when you write. The remarks that follow may offer some helpful strategies as you work with the essays in this reader.

The Essay

It is far easier to say what the essay is *not* than to say what it is; it is not a poem or drama or catalogue or lab report or any one of a long list of other forms of writing we might cite. But definition by negation does not help much, nor does a definition such as Aldous Huxley's flippant "The essay is a literary device for saying almost everything about anything." One way to define the essay is to describe it as "a brief prose composition that attempts to make and develop an assertion in an engaging manner." It is worth pausing to consider the different elements of this definition. First, the essay is brief, perhaps only a few typed pages. Second, the essay is prose. Alexander Pope referred to his verse compositions, the "Essay on Criticism" and the "Essay on Man," as essays, but few writers since the eighteenth century have followed his example. Essays today are works of nonfiction in prose. Third, the essay writer attempts to develop an assertion, to make one point clearly and effectively. Finally, the word "essay," from the French noun *essai*, an "attempt," reflects the view of Michel de Montaigne, a sixteenth-century French philosopher and creator of the "essai." Montaigne considered his essays attempts to respond to a wide variety of issues and events in a thoughtful, somewhat personal way.

One way to classify essays in general is to distinguish the formal essay from the informal essay. The formal essay most often presents a serious subject for a specialized audience; its author writes as an acknowledged authority whose purpose is to inform the reader; the tone of the formal essay tends to be impersonal. Nancy Sommers's "Revision Strategies of Student Writers and Experienced Adult Writers," Niccolò Machiavelli's "The Morals of the Prince," and Jean-Paul Sartre's "Existentialism" illustrate the formal essay. The informal essay, on the other hand, deals with events from everyday life and presents its subject matter for a general reader; its author is often a keen observer or participant who writes in a personal way. Examples of informal essays in *The Norton Reader* include Dylan Thomas's "Memories of Christmas," Daniel Mark Epstein's "The Case of Harry Houdini," and Phyllis Rose's "Shopping and Other Spiritual Adventures."

Every essay, whether formal or informal, focuses attention on a particular subject and seeks to make a definite point for a specific audience. It is a combination of objective elements and subjective responses. In writing essays in college, keep in mind the importance of balancing personal response with objective material. You limit the effectiveness of your writing when the reader is left with the impression that all you have written is opinion.

Rhetoric and the Modes of Essay Writing

When you hear someone's remarks dismissed as "mere rhetoric," you know that the term is less than glowing: the speaker or writer may have mastered the means of expression–style and delivery–but is found lacking in substance. Politicians often face this charge. Yet *rhetoric* also has positive meaning, for it refers to both knowledge and skill of strategies for effective communication. Aristotle's *Rhetoric* is the central document in the study of rhetoric. For Aristotle, rhetoric has mostly to do with persuasion, with inventing arguments, arranging evidence, and expressing ideas in aptly chosen language. For our purpose, rhetoric is the knowledge of the skills and strategies needed to communicate ideas, with grace and fluency, to a designated audience.

Rhetorical tradition provides a convenient way of distinguishing one type of essay from another; we can speak of four basic "modes" or types of essay writing: narrative, descriptive, expository, and argumentative. Narrative essays, which relate an event or a series of events, demonstrate a particular dimension of the storyteller's art: creating a story from factual, material. Unlike a short story or novel or fable, narrative essays deal exclusively with "real world" events. Descriptive essays create impressions that appeal to our senses. Expository essays offer explanations, most often by supplying substantial information presented in a logical manner. Among the most common forms of exposition, which can also be called analysis, are essays of comparison/contrast, classification, definition, process analysis, and causal analysis. Finally, argumentative essays seek to convince the reader of the correctness of a particular point of view. Strictly speaking, argument and persuasion are two different activities (argument appeals to reason and seeks assent; persuasion appeals to emotion and seeks action), but they are often combined in effective writing. Likewise, while it is possible to write an essay that is pure narrative or pure description or pure exposition, it is much more likely that you will mix modes in your own writing.

Writing as Process

The composing process involves all stages of your work, from the first ideas you have or notes you jot down through the presentation of the final copy. It extends well beyond the physical acts of putting pen to paper or hands to keyboard, for, in the process of composing –in reading, reflecting, discussing, and writing–you are actively involved in creating a text.

Consider the kinds of writing activities you might use in working on an essay: preliminary writing (notes, journal entries, freewriting); inventing a thesis and designing an essay (trial thesis statements and outlines); working up a draft; revising, editing the best draft for final copy. Seen in this way, writing is a process by and through which you can progress from tentative responses and jottings to a final draft worthy of submission.

Writing is also a cognitive process, a means by which you learn more about a particular subject, about other people, and about yourself. At no point will you or any writer know everything about a specific topic, but in most cases you will know more by the time you submit the final copy than you did when you invented your thesis or wrote your first draft. The status of writing as a cognitive process means two things for you. First, you can expect to learn from your writing. And second, you can be confident that your writing will improve with effort, for you and the essay are "in process" toward a goal.

Reading and Writing

Reading and writing might seem to be opposing activities. Careful reading calls for analysis, splitting a text apart in order to understand how it is constructed. Effective writing, on the other hand, demands synthesis, binding elements together so that they function as a whole. Yet reading and writing are complementary activities, for the better you understand how a given essay "works," the more you learn about how to make your own writing "work."

In considering anything you have read, you need to ask yourself two important questions, both of them posed by a distinguished teacher, Robert Scholes: What does this text mean? How does it mean? When you have finished reading, you will have some tentative responses; when you have discussed the reading in class, you will have clearer answers; and when you have written your essay, you will have significantly deepened your understanding of the text. Put another way, writing will complete the experience of reading.

How to Read: Some Practical Suggestions

A good understanding of any serious essay requires more than just one reading. You might adopt a three-part method of reading your assigned essays: first, an uninterrupted narrative reading to acquire a basic sense of the text (What does it mean?); then, a close, analytical, annotated reading to appreciate the structure and logic of the text (How does it mean?); finally, a "review reading" to synthesize your earlier readings. Because careful reading is analysis, you will want to be precise as you examine all the elements–even the title–of the essays you read.

As you read, annotate your text with a free but directed hand. Underline important ideas and essential terms; underline passages you do not understand; put question marks and comments in the margins. Imagine that you are in conversation with the writer and respond accordingly. If a particular idea strikes you as insightful, make a note. If the writer's thought seems unclear, note that you want to focus on it in your next reading or in discussion. Refer to your annotated text in class to remind you what ideas provoked you and where you had questions. Use your annotation to bring your personal perspective and experience to bear on what you read. This is an essential part of the composing process.

What to Look for When You Read

To get at the structure and substance of an essay, spend some time considering the following elements:

1. *Title, and Opening and Closing Paragraphs*

Notice the title–it can be an important aspect of the essay, serving to catch the reader's interest and sometimes giving a clear indication of what the essay is about. Study the opening paragraph, a vital part of an essay, one which establishes some common ground with the reader. The opening paragraph often articulates the thesis of the essay. Take a look at how Brent Staples in "Black Men and Public Space" and Betty Rollin in "Motherhood: Who Needs It?" startle the reader in their opening paragraphs. Consider the closing paragraph. It should reinforce the thesis and offer an assessment, an observation, or a prediction; it should leave the reader with something to think about. Look at the provocative closing paragraphs of "Decolonizing the Mind" by Ngũgĩ wa Thiong'o and "Shopping and Other Spiritual Adventures" by Phyllis Rose.

2. *Thesis, Development, and Support*

Examine the essay for a thesis statement, a sentence in which the writer takes a stand and indicates his or her central purpose. Sometimes, as in Judith Viorst's "Good as Guilt," the writer's thesis is explicitly stated. Other times, as in E. B. White's "Once More to the Lake," where there is probably no single sentence that will satisfactorily represent the entire essay, the writer implies it. In such cases the careful reader should be able to construct a thesis statement.

How does the writer develop the main idea of the essay? Sometimes a thesis will rest on assumptions, related ideas that the writer does not mention directly but expects the reader to understand or to agree to or, if the real purpose is deception, to overlook. Machiavelli, in "The Morals of the Prince," appears to assume that it is more important for a prince to stay in power than to be a "good" man. In considering what you read, always ask yourself: What assumptions has the writer made? Apply that question to Elisabeth Kübler-Ross's "On the Fear of Death" or Stephen Jay Gould's "The Terrifying Normalcy of AIDS."

How does the writer support the main idea of the essay? Determine what kinds of support have been enlisted. Factual evidence (material easily verifiable or attested to by reliable witnesses) or opinion? If opinion, whose? That of a recognized authority? Furthermore, consider whether or not the support is sufficient for the subject, purpose, and audience. Is the evidence appropriate and convincing? Evaluate the evidence Anthony Burgess draws on in his essay "Is America Falling Apart?"

3. *Organization*

A well-written essay is clearly, logically, and carefully organized. Its skeletal structure can be discerned, removed, and examined. Think of this process as something like boning a fish: if the essay has been organized well, you should be able to delineate its structure as easily as you can separate the skeletal system from a freshly caught trout. As an exercise in discerning structure, see if you can "bone" George Orwell's "Shooting an Elephant" or Desmond Morris's "Territorial Behavior."

4. *Persona*

When you read an essay, you should be able to form an impression of the writer from the text. In response to choices of subject, purpose, and, most importantly, audience, the writer creates a particular image. Elements like tone, word choice, figures of speech, sentence complexity, and paragraph length–that is, the writer's "style"–create a persona. Your response to the writer's persona is of crucial importance, particularly in argument, where, if the writer fails to create a persona that is fair, knowledgeable, and trustworthy, the argument is lost. You should be able to characterize the writer's persona. One way to do this is to draw up a short list of adjectives that describe the voice you heard in the essay you read. Try this exercise on Margaret Atwood's "Writing the Male Character" or Eudora Welty's "One Writer's Beginnings."

Upon completion of your close reading, you should be able to summarize the essay as a whole, describe the strategies the writer has used, and offer your view of the success or failure of the essay by pointing to specific elements in the text.

How to Write: Some Suggestions Based upon Reading

Through reading, you sharpen your sense of what a good essay is. You develop an awareness of the elements that determine its success or failure, taking into consideration title, opening and closing paragraphs, thesis, development and support, and persona. Now your work as a writer begins. The nine brief points that follow are suggestions for developing your understanding of writing.

1. Have something to say. You can know all the fine points of form and style, but unless you have discovered something to say, there is no sense in writing.
2. Know your subject. Review your annotated text and class notes.
3. Articulate your purpose. If it has not been assigned in class, determine it for yourself.
4. Develop a clear sense of your audience. Ask yourself two questions: For whom am I writing this? What must I do to communicate successfully with my reader? Develop a clear sense of your own voice–know your persona.
5. Once you have these four aspects defined, formulate a thesis statement that expresses the central idea of your essay. Use whatever method works for you–freewriting, brainstorming, cataloguing responses to what you have read–but put your thesis, however tentative, in writing.
6. Design your essay by drawing up an outline to guide its development.

7. Write a rough draft. Go ahead and write, no matter what you think of the quality. A first draft, however rough, gives you something to work with.

8. Revise the draft. "Re-see" your essay in light of its subject, purpose, and audience. Examine its design. Judge how effectively it supports its central thesis.

9. Edit your revised draft. Proofread your final essay.

PERSONAL REPORT

DYLAN THOMAS

Memories of Christmas

(The Norton Reader, p. 1; Shorter Edition, p. 1)

Dylan Thomas's "Memories of Christmas" opens "Personal Report" with a nostalgic look at the poet's childhood in Wales. An essay resonant with poetic description, it mixes impressions of Christmas with recollections of particular Christmases gone by. To Thomas's poetic gifts are added his talent for character analysis and his ear for dialogue and song, whether actual lyrics or the tune created by words.

Analytical Considerations

1. Re: content
   a. Who is Mrs. Potter?
   b. For whom is the teddy bear named?
   c. What does "bombilating" mean?
   d. At whose house was the fire one Christmas?
   e. Name two of the boys who went "padding through the streets" with the author one Christmas Day afternoon.

2. Discuss the power of description in "Memories of Christmas." Have students point out passages where Thomas's description is particularly vivid. Discuss the techniques he draws on: metaphor, simile, hyphenation, etc.

3. Read the essay aloud to explore further how Thomas infuses prose with the techniques of poetry. This may be the best way for students to appreciate the rhythm and sound patterns that give "Memories of Christmas" its richness.

4. Direct attention to the ways by which Thomas unifies the essay. Two prominent examples are the metaphor of the snowball and the persona of the child. Have students trace the progress of the metaphor and discuss its function. Concerning persona, point out that though Thomas succeeds in re-creating the world of childhood experience, certain clues tell us that the essay is a *re*-creation. How do we know that "Memories of Childhood" was written by an adult? Consider such clues as description unavailable to a child (. . . "Mrs. Prothero was announcing ruin like a town-crier in Pompeii") and understated humor ("Bank the gong and call the fire-brigade and the book-loving firemen!").

5. Thomas's use of voice(s) is important here, from the "voices I sometimes hear" (paragraph 1) to the "small, dry voice" from the

other side of the door at the end of the essay. Distinguish among the voices; how does Thomas orchestrate them?

Suggested Writing Assignments

1. Write an essay on the power of language in "Memories of Christmas."

2. Use Thomas's essay as a model for writing your own recollection of childhood. Do not concern yourself (as Thomas does not) with historical accuracy; rather, aim to make your description fresh and vivid.

3. Write an essay about the meaning and value of nostalgia. What is nostalgia? Use a dictionary definition, perhaps the *Oxford English Dictionary* entry, as your starting point.

WALLACE STEGNER

The Town Dump

The Norton Reader, p. 10; Shorter Edition, p. 6

In another essay of childhood recollection Wallace Stegner shares with Dylan Thomas a desire to use memory as a retrieval system, but his interests are personal as well as historical. His essay differs from Thomas's in purpose and strategy. Stegner has added commentary, reflection upon his observations, to his essay, and we are always aware that the writer is a mature man narrating and commenting. The closing three paragraphs elaborate the thesis Stegner has introduced at the very beginning: "it [the town dump] has more poetry and excitement in it than people did."

Analytical Considerations

1. Re: content:
   a. Where was the town dump?
   b. What did old Mrs. Gustafson find on her way home from the dump?
   c. The skeleton of what animal that had belonged to Stegner was found in the dump?
   d. Who owned the volumes of Shakespeare found there?
   e. Identify lares and penates; kitchen midden.

2. Ask students to consider the structure and organization of this essay. Work through the essay, paragraph by paragraph, and let them tell how each functions. Direct their attention to transitional elements and shifts (e.g., at paragraphs 9, 17, 19). This essay combines narrative and commentary; how is structure related to purpose here?

3. An important strategy in this essay is Stegner's early mention of something that turns out to be important later. Students should note this in at least two instances: the thesis at the end of paragraph 1 and the "skeleton of the boy's pet colt" in paragraph 11. In each case Stegner's development emphasizes the importance of the idea. Moreover, his technique is related to his sense of audience; it is elementary, but students may need to have the point reinforced.

4. In any terms you think appropriate, ask students to compare and contrast this essay with Dylan Thomas's "Memories of Christmas" (NR 1, SE 1).

5. Have students cull Stegner's references to poetry and get a sense of what "poetry" does, as far as he is concerned. Then ask how poetry is like the town dump.

6. Return to Stegner's conclusion at the end of paragraph 1: "it [the town dump] has more poetry and excitement in it than people did." Have students focus on the verbs here; when they note that the first is in the present tense and the second in the past, let that observation open your discussion of this essay. Two central questions should arise: What does Stegner mean by "poetry"? Why is it that his insight is gained in the present moment of writing the essay rather than the past moment of actually visiting the town dump?

Suggested Writing Assignments

1. Expand responses to Analytical Consideration 4 into an essay.

2. Is there any place in your house–the attic, the cellar, your room–that might provide you with the raw material to write an essay like Stegner's? If so, write it.

3. Write an essay about a dump (or any other place given to the disposal of unwanted items) as "a symbol of how much was lost, how much thrown aside, how much carelessly or of necessity given up, in the making of a new country."

4. Write an essay in response to what Stegner says in his last paragraph: "For a community may be as well judged by what it throws away–what it has to throw away and what it chooses to–as by any other evidence." ("Civilization" or "culture" might be substituted for "community.")

Additional questions on this essay will be found in the text (NR 15, SE 10).

MAYA ANGELOU

Graduation

The Norton Reader, p. 22; Shorter Edition, p. 11

Maya Angelou's essay "Graduation," taken from the first volume of her autobiography, *I Know Why the Caged Bird Sings*, is a fluent and powerful example of personal experience narration. In its concern to recapture the world of a child as well as in its attention to poetry and to the use of poetic technique and in its structure, "Graduation" invites comparison with Wallace Stegner's "The Town Dump." Angelou's approach to the subject of her essay is more typical of personal narratives and is perhaps less sophisticated than Stegner's. For instance, the difference between the two essays in structure–determined largely by subject matter–is readily apparent. Angelou writes about a certain event or a series of related events which happen within a determinable period of time. Therefore, the essay can be a straightforward narrative, organized chronologically. Stegner's use of spatial organization reflects his more complex subject. Such relationship as there is between the events he describes was not apparent to Stegner as they happened. Also, as the events are replayed in the mind of the author, the location in time of one doesn't necessarily suggest when another must have occurred.

Other bases for comparison of the two essays which may be investigated include: (1) the types of concrete details Stegner and Angelou use and the effectiveness of these details; (2) the relative success with which each author reproduces the thoughts and feelings of a child; (3) the extent in each essay to which the experience itself is allowed to convey ideas, attitudes, and feelings; (4) the conclusions of the essays, for both Stegner and Angelou draw general observations from their particular experiences.

Analytical Considerations

1. Re: content
   a. Name the town and state in which "Graduation" takes place.
   b. Name two ways by which Angelou classifies students.
   c. In what year did Angelou graduate from eighth grade?
   d. Who was the graduation speaker, and what was the theme of his address?
   e. What was Maya Angelou's name at the time?

2. Have students examine the structure of "Graduation." How does the opening paragraph function? How long does it take Angelou to get to the actual event? What has she done in that space? Ask someone to pinpoint the place in the text where Angelou's tone changes. How does that signal a change not only in tone but also in content and rhetoric? Follow through to the end with that analysis.

3. Angelou is a woman of many accomplishments, among them successful work as poet and songwriter. Students could profitably examine "Graduation" for its use of poetry and poetic devices–simile, metaphor, and rhythm–to get started. In the concluding paragraphs she speaks about the function of poetry, but what is "poetry" for her? Clearly this leads to comparisons with Dylan Thomas and Wallace Stegner.

4. Why did Angelou write "Graduation"? For whom did she write it?

5. Ask students to consider what it means to say that "Graduation" was composed by a writer doubly oppressed. Ask if they can tell that this was written by a woman. How? What indications are there of a particular culture, time, and person?

Suggested Writing Assignments

1. In terms of content, technique, purpose, and audience, compare/contrast "Graduation" with "Memories of Christmas" and "The Town Dump."

2. Write an account of the events narrated in "Graduation" from Mr. Donleavy's perspective.

3. "Graduation" is a cultural as well as personal and literary document. Write an essay about its place and value in American cultural history. What does it say? What does it *not* say?

4. The theme of great expectations fulfilled or unfulfilled has been used time and again in literature. Does that theme offer a way of writing about something of your own experience? If so, write about it.

HUGH MACLENNAN

On Living in a Cold Country

The Shorter Edition, p. 21

In "On Living in a Cold Country," Hugh MacLennan brings to light in an arch manner one of the most common assumptions about Canada. He writes the kind of duty piece, "heavy on the snow and the cold," that he seems to disdain when he talks about it in the essay. What MacLennan does, however, is turn convention around. While snow and cold temperatures are crucial elements in MacLennan's witty essay, they are not the antagonists they seem to be in most Canadian duty pieces. We find no Mounties and trappers contending with the elements for their very survival. Instead, we find a little boy surviving–quite nicely, thank you–in a tent in sub-zero weather, cheerfully and easily adapting to the elements; it is never too snowy or cold for him in that notoriously wintry place Halifax,

Nova Scotia. Thus, Hugh MacLennan mildly parodies Canadian duty pieces in "On Living in a Cold Country." His gentle reproof of the typical American's smug, conventional view of Canada is a reminder to us all that stereotypical views of any kind are by nature erroneous; in becoming convention, they are removed from the level of actual life.

Analytical Considerations

1. Re: content
   a. Who is the "ship-met" writer? What does MacLennan learn from him?
   b. Why is Canada a cold country?
   c. How does the cold become "high poetry"?
   d. Why is MacLennan destined to be a writer?
2. Describe the characteristics of the persona that emerge from this essay. Does MacLennan seem to have a humorous distance from himself? What details reveal that distance?
3. Do you find irony in this essay? Consider this early sentence: "I had worked and played hard, and had been equipping myself for twentieth-century life by studying Latin and Greek." Is it ironic? What other statements or events in the essay are ironic?
4. What gives unity to this essay? The focus on the stereotypical image of Canada? Is the material about the author's becoming a writer a framing device for the essay or the main point of the essay? Explain your answer.
5. Though in much of the essay MacLennan presents himself as the naïve or ignorant person in discussions–between him and the ship-met writer, between him and the editor–is this presentation disingenuous? Is the reader supposed to see that in fact, these other people are naïve, ignorant, or stupid? What are the clues that this is so?

Suggested Writing Assignments

1. Hugh MacLennan suggests the folly of thinking in stereotypes, but is there anything worthwhile about conventional or stereotypical views? Write an essay about the uses and dangers of stereotypes.
2. Defend or refute, in an essay, these statements:

   "In the entire history of the human race, no important art has ever come out of a cold country."

   "Canada is a cold country because that's what the world believes it is."
3. Think about the Freudian analysis of young MacLennan

offered by the ship-met writer. Then write an essay about the necessary qualities of a writer.

Additional questions on this essay will be found in the text (SE 28).

RICHARD HUGO

How I Never Met Eudora Welty

The Norton Reader, p. 32, Shorter Edition, p. 29

Richard Hugo's ability to sketch character with several deft strokes and create an appealing persona enables him to give new life to a well-worn topic, the autobiographical essay about life in high school. Essentially "How I Never Met Eudora Welty" is a study of four characters: Logan The Finger, H. Reed Fulton, Grant Redford, and Richard Hugo. This tale of Hugo's coming-of-age as a writer is told with humor, irony, and some degree of self-deprecation. Hugo's rendering of the high school experience should appeal to students, indeed to all of us who have been through it, no matter when.

Analytical Considerations

1. Re: content
   a. What high school did Hugo attend?
   b. Who was the principal?
   c. Why didn't Hugo attend college until 1945?
   d. Only when he concentrated his energies on what did Hugo begin to realize the only reward of writing?
   e. Why didn't Hugo ever meet Eudora Welty?
2. Have students determine the organizational principles and structure of the essay.What happens with the paragraph that begins "I graduated in 1941"?
3. Ask students to choose and analyze the most effective scene in this essay. How do they account for Hugo's success? Persona? Humor?
4. Why did Hugo want to meet Welty? What did his not meeting her teach him? How does the title function here?

Suggested Writing Assignments

1. Write about the experience of high school. Describe the person "most likely to be remembered" and explain why. Or write about a place that has stuck in your head: study hall, backstage of the theater, baseball dugout.

2. Write an essay about how a negative became a positive for you--how not meeting someone or not getting something you wanted turned out to be beneficial.

Additional questions on this essay will be found in the text (NR 35, SE 32).

HANS A. SCHMITT

January 30, 1933: A Memoir

The Norton Reader, p. 36, Shorter Edition, p. 33

Hans A. Schmitt's memoir, written with clarity and economy, documents a boy's rite of passage. The events of January 30, 1933, had an irreversible effect on him and his family, to say nothing of German society. That fifty years later Schmitt has chosen to record what happened then testifies to the impact of the day's events. He gives us a convincing sketch of a teenage boy, creating a character whose attitudes will enable some students to see something of themselves. In effect, "January 30, 1933" is more than a memoir; it is a study of how larger political events affect the development of individuals and the life of the family.

Analytical Considerations

1. Re: content
   a. What is the German equivalent of crossing fingers for good luck?
   b. What famous American novel, in translation, did Schmitt read on his day off?
   c. Hans's mother and Fritz's father had what in common?
   d. Who was president of the German republic when Hitler became chancellor?
   e. What effect did the political news of January 30, 1933, have on the Schmitt family?

2. Spend some time on the rhetorical qualities of this memoir, particularly its narrative design and persona. Have students divide the essay into its two basic parts and determine the structure of each.

3. You might want to caution students about forming generalizations on limited evidence before considering the memoir as a cultural document. What does it reveal about a particular family in Germany in January 1933? What does it reveal about the relationship between parents and children? Between siblings? Between husband and wife?

4. Have students observe how Schmitt uses the symbol of the door, open as well as closed. First, ask that they note each time the

door appears in the narrative section with a sense of how it functions on a literal level; then ask them to note how Schmitt uses the door as metaphor in the last two paragraphs.

5. This essay takes its particular focus from language. Seen as a dramatic piece, it reaches a climax with the father's use of an expletive in front of his children. Ask students to explain the place of that "expletive scene" in the dramatic structure of the memoir.

6. One of the most interesting aspects of "January 30, 1933" concerns its value as a record of a rite of passage. Ask students to chart the emotional growth of the boy Hans.

7. How does the adult Hans Schmitt view the experience of this day from his perspective fifty years later? Why did he write this memoir?

Suggested Writing Assignments

1. If a historical event has had an important role in changing the patterns of your own life, write an essay about it.

2. Both Hans and Fritz lived in two worlds, one German, the other Jewish; we know that they would be alienated and excluded even more as Hitler solidified his power. Though perhaps not in such catastrophic terms, many people have experienced these same feelings. Write an essay about the causes and effects of being an "outsider" in any context you wish.

3. Write an account of the events narrated in "January 30, 1933" from the perspective of Hans's mother.

BRUNO BETTELHEIM

A Victim

The Norton Reader, p. 41, Shorter Edition, p. 58

This excerpt from Bettelheim's highly praised study of his experiences as a prisoner of the Gestapo *The Informed Heart* offers distilled insight into an episode that occurred nearly twenty years before Dr. Bettelheim wrote the account. A renowned psychologist, Bettelheim writes with clarity and detachment about his experience in a German concentration camp during World War II. From his dealings with an SS man assigned to determine those prisoners who would receive medical attention and those who would not, Bettelheim learned an important truth about persecutors and victims: Refusal to act in accordance with the stereotype of the victim held by the persecutor may grant the former some relief. Persecution ceased when Bettelheim refused to play the role expected of him; his matter-of-fact attitude and stoic endurance of pain earned the respect of his persecutor.

Analytical Considerations

1. Re: content
   a. Briefly describe the episode narrated by Bettelheim.
   b. Why did others resent Bettelheim's attitude toward the SS man?
   c. Why did Bettelheim succeed where others failed?
   d. What was the privilege extended to Bettelheim?
   e. Approximately how long after the experience did Bettelheim write this?

2. Ask students to analyze the first paragraph in terms of its function and in terms of its structure. Do the five sentences that constitute the paragraph move in a particular direction? Toward what? How does paragraph 2 function? Discuss the last two paragraphs of the essay, not only as a conclusion but also as a unit in the three-part design of the essay.

3. Students may need to be reminded that Bettelheim is extrapolating here; from one episode in his own life he has drawn what he considers a truth about human behavior. It is important for students to see how much depends on assumptions in this piece. Do students accept that Bettelheim is presenting a truth about human behavior, or do they think that his experience merely illustrates the principle that some people are born lucky?

4. The opening paragraph makes it clear that Bettelheim intends this lesson to be applied to other contexts. Do your students think that he is correct? If so, to what situations might it be applicable?

Suggested Writing Assignments

1. Write an essay in response to Analytical Consideration 4 above.

2. Write an essay designed with the same three-part structure as Bettelheim's, only from the perspective of the SS officer. Try to account for his change in conduct, and perhaps attitude, toward prisoner Bettelheim.

3. Compare/contrast Willard Gaylin's sense of human personality in "What You See Is the Real You" (NR 664, SE 386) with Bettelheim's.

4. Consider whether or not Bettelheim's insight might have any validity for Maya Angelou ("Graduation" [NR 22, SE 11]), James Baldwin ("Stranger in the Village" [NR 547]), or Martin Luther King, Jr. ("Letter from Birmingham Jail" [NR 792, SE 473]).

JOAN DIDION

On Going Home

The Norton Reader, p. 69, Shorter Edition, p. 40

In a short, six-paragraph essay Joan Didion describes the experience of returning to her family's home to celebrate her daughter's first birthday. Her husband remains in Los Angeles, and she reenters the world of her father, mother, brother, and great-aunts. "On Going Home" is Didion's notebook of the experience, an intensely visual record of a visit that prompted her to think about several questions: What is "home"? Can you go home again? How does memory work? Didion's essay confronts an essential truth of human existence: You cannot escape your past. In addition, it confirms what she advises in "On Keeping a Notebook" (NR 731, SE 414): "to keep on nodding terms with the people we used to be. . . ."

Analytical Considerations

1. What does "home" mean to Didion?
2. What does she mean by the "vital although troublesome distinction" between home as the place where she lives with her husband and baby in Los Angeles and home as the place where her family lives in the Central Valley of California?
3. Didion ends her first paragraph with a short sentence: "Marriage is the classic betrayal." What does it mean? Whose idea is it? Didion's?
4. Like the other essays by Didion in the *Reader*, "On Going Home" displays Joan Didion's ability to work with and through striking visual images. Let students discuss several here and comment on their effect.
5. Do students, like Didion, "find in family life the source of all tension and drama"?
6. What is the significance of the "young girl on crystal" in paragraph 2?
7. Why doesn't Didion discard any of the items in the drawer she decides to clean out?
8. How does the vandalized graveyard function in this essay?
9. Why did Didion give her daughter a xylophone and a sundress?
10. Ask students how "On Going Home" functions as an essay. Let them examine it for standard elements of thesis, development, support, organization, etc. Ask if there is movement or direction discernible. Unity? (Why does Didion return to the baby's birthday at the end?)

Comparative Considerations

1. Compare "On Going Home" with "On Keeping a Notebook" not only in terms of rhetoric and style but in terms of process as well. How do objects function within the narrative? How do images function? Does an image of stringing beads together make sense as a way of talking about Didion's prose style?

2. Is there a characteristic Didion persona in the four essays in the *Reader*? Describe it; then analyze how it is developed and used.

Suggested Writing Assignments

1. Write an essay comparing/contrasting Joan Didion's experience in returning home with that of Joyce Maynard ("Four Generations" [SE 43]).

2. In one way, this is an essay about the significance of keeping objects of particular meaning with us. Didion's drawer contains a number of these objects; the gift–seemingly incongruous and inappropriate–of a xylophone for a one-year old child may assume such a role for her daughter. If you have kept a collection of objects for the same purpose, write an essay about their significance and function in your life.

3. Write an essay in response to Didion's assertion that "in family life [lies] the source of all tension and drama."

Additional questions on this essay will be found in the text (NR 72, SE 42).

JOYCE MAYNARD

Four Generations

Shorter Edition, p. 40

Many of the essays in the "Personal Report" section suggest how time and place and events give us a way to view the world and a sense of belonging in the world. Joyce Maynard's "Four Generations," like Joan Didion's "On Going Home" (NR 69, SE 40), suggests how family is a primary source of sight and security for the individual.

Her grandmother's dying provokes Maynard to consider her familial connections and relationships. There are obvious conflicts, frustrated expectations, thwarted desires in all such relations, the "ambushes of family life," Didion calls them. But Maynard comes to perceive what is stronger but less obvious: the bonds between generations; family rituals that are repeated unwittingly because they provide a sort of comfort and security; unqualified, if sometimes smothering, love. Such bonds and rituals and love are inescapable; they shape us and give us meaning. The dying of her grandmother has given Joyce Maynard, with benevolent irony, an insight about what sustains life.

Analytical Considerations

1. Re: content
   a. What is the grandmother's family background?
   b. Why did Maynard resent her grandmother?
   c. How did Audrey respond to her great-grandmother?
   d. What is the significance of the lamb coat?

2. Stories revolving around the deaths of loved ones are often sentimental, overwritten, and bathetic. How does Maynard escape such sentimentalism? What elevates her essay beyond personal lamentations?

3. "Four Generations" is quite brief. Are you able, however, to get a picture of each of the four generations, especially of Maynard's grandmother? Explain Maynard's technique of quickly giving a few telling details that reveal the grandmother's life and person. Is the technique successful?

4. Does the ending of "Four Generations" offer a sense of continuity in life, the sense that the life cycle repeats itself through the generations? Is such a sense of continuity perhaps the consolation Maynard has as she loses her grandmother?

5. Explain the statement "Every one of those mothers loves and needs her daughter more than her daughter will love or need her some day. . . ." Do you think it a true observation of the way most mother-daughter relationships are?

Suggested Writing Assignments

1. Write an essay about some element or relationship in your family life that is important. Use Maynard's approach of developing concrete details and examples.

2. Write an essay comparing what Joyce Maynard has to say about family and home with what Joan Didion ("On Going Home") has to say on these subjects. What common realizations do they seem to come to?

3. Write an essay about some element or relationship in your family life that is important. Use Maynard's approach of developing by concrete details and examples.

4. What is your attitude toward allowing the grandmother to die without life-prolonging surgery? Do you support passive euthanasia (not using extraordinary life-support systems)? Active euthanasia (administering a drug, for example, that would put a disease victim out of his or her misery)? Write an essay expressing your opinion.

LOREN EISELEY

The Brown Wasps

The Norton Reader, p. 72, Shorter Edition, p. 46

This is not the last time that we will encounter a scientist who is also a superb prose stylist. A poet as well as an anthropologist, Loren Eiseley writes a carefully structured and compelling statement of the significance of personal memory and the influence of the past on the present. Drawing on examples from nature and from his own experience, Eiseley points up the tremendous value we place on memories as objects of "permanence" in a confusing, changeable world.

Analytical Considerations

1. Re: content
   a. In the opening paragraph, what forms of life does Eiseley compare to wasps?
   b. Eiseley's observation of what creature caused him to look "with sudden care and attention at things [he] had been running over thoughtlessly for years"?
   c. For what creatures was the old Philadelphia elevated railway "a food-bearing river"?
   d. As a boy Eiseley planted what kind of tree in Nebraska?
   e. How many years later did Eiseley return to Nebraska?

2. It is important to have students consider the power of Eiseley's observations. Ask students if he has followed his own intention to look "with sudden care and attention at things I had been running over thoughtlessly for years."

3. Students need to appreciate how Eiseley's inductive method works here. You might illuminate the process thus:
   a. Have students mark passages of narration and observation, distinguishing them from passages of ideas.
   b. Next, discuss each of the examples of living creatures in action to show how Eiseley arrives at his ideas inductively. (What do his description of brown wasps and his observations of the field mouse and pigeons have to do with his purpose?)
   c. Ask if students can locate an explicit thesis statement; if not, ask them to construct an adequate and appropriate one, then to determine how Eiseley's inductive method develops his thesis.

4. Several passages present significant opportunities for discussion. Consider assigning them in advance.
   a. Paragraph 7: "You want your place in the hive more than you want a room or a place where the aged can be eased

gently out of the way. It is the place that matters, the place at the heart of things. It is life that you want, that bruises your gray old head with the hard chairs; a man has a right to his place."

b. Paragraph 25: "After sixty years the mood of the brown wasps grows heavier upon one."
c. Paragraph 36: "I spoke for myself, one field mouse, and several pigeons. We were all out of touch but somehow permanent. It was the world that had changed."

Suggested Writing Assignments

1. On the basis of your observations of a particular animal, say, a dog or a cat or a horse, write an essay that works by induction and develops an analogy in connection with human behavior.
2. If you have ever returned to a place that was once home and experienced the shock of dislocation or the trauma of disappearance, write an essay about the episode.
3. Write an essay on the need among creatures, all creatures, to "cling to a time and place."

Additional questions on this essay will be found in the text (NR 78, SE 52).

E. B. WHITE

Once More to the Lake

The Norton Reader, p. 79, Shorter Edition, p. 53

"Once More to the Lake" is a classic essay on mortality. Though the subject is sobering, if not somber, E. B. White never allows pessimism or depression to color his reflections. Set within a natural context of land- and waterscape, White's narrative appears to be natural as well. Easy and graceful, with fluent transition and discernible unity, it is a metaphor for the substance of this master craftsman's thought. The natural cycle of life passing from one generation to the next is carefully recorded through the eyes of a man who recalls childhood impressions with clarity while confronting his own mortality.

Analytical Considerations

1. Ask students if "Once More to the Lake" has a thesis statement; then ask if it has a theme. Why do narrative essays often have a "theme" rather than a "thesis"?

2. Comparison/contrast is probably White's most important rhetorical strategy here. Ask students where and how he uses it.
3. Ask students to consider how paragraph 8 differs from the previous seven. What is its function in relation to the whole essay?
4. Let students speculate about why White created that long sentence in paragraph 8. What effect does it have?
5. You might want students to spend some time accounting for the success of White's description of the thunderstorm in paragraph 12.
6. Discuss the persona White creates in "Once More to the Lake." Ask what textual clues enable the reader to construct an image of the writer.
7. How does the last sentence function? Does it come as a surprise?

Comparative Considerations

Certainly "Once More to the Lake" reveals aspects of E. B. White familiar to readers of "Some Remarks on Humor" (NR 1076, SE 663), "Democracy" (NR 833, SE 514), and "Progress and Change" (NR 375, SE 258). Yet it differs from the other three pieces. How? in expected or unexpected ways? Are these "revelations" evidence of White's flexibility and range, or are they different E. B. Whites?

Suggested Writing Assignment

If you have had the opportunity to revisit a cherished place from childhood, write an essay on the experience. Where does "change" lie? In a place? In you? Did the experience lead you to sober reflection on big issues? If so, structure your essay so that you can include commentary as well as narrative/description/exposition.

Additional questions on this essay will be found in the text (NR 84, SE 58).

PEOPLE, PLACES

MARGARET MEAD

Home and Travel

Shorter Edition, p. 59

A serious scholar and seminal figure in the relatively new science of anthropology, Margaret Mead was, by the end of her life, familiar to most Americans. Many had read her scientific and theoretical works–*Coming of Age in Samoa* or *Male and Female*, for instance–because Dr. Mead wrote for a lay as well as professional audience. In this regard she antedated such contemporary scientist-popular writers as Carl Sagan, Isaac Asimov, Lewis Thomas, Elisabeth Kübler-Ross, and Stephen Jay Gould (all of whom are represented in *The Norton Reader*). Millions of other Americans came to know Dr. Mead through her television appearances, in which she applied her studies of other cultures to issues in contemporary American society, managing always to be provocative, if not controversial. Dr. Mead's availability to the general public made her an unusual scientist; her life and views made her an unusual woman of her time –an important early feminist.

"Home and Travel" is taken from Margaret Mead's autobiographical best seller *Blackberry Winter*. It is not an anthropological piece, but Dr. Mead's researches among faraway cultures are reflected in several examples near the end of the essay. As Dr. Mead wrote in the Acknowledgments to *Blackberry Winter*, "Although the focus . . . is not on [the peoples of her research], they are nonetheless present. . . ."

Analytical Considerations

1. Re: content
    a. No matter where Mead's family moved, they always came home to______________.
    b. Name one of the objects her mother kept on her dressing table.
    c. What do Kalahari Bushmen use to make a doorway when they camp in the desert?
    d. What European country does Mead call a "widow's walk"?
    e. What is Mead's daughter's name?
2. You might ask students to analyze Mead's prose. Choose a paragraph, and ask them to study her sentences for length, type, variation, and punctuation. Choose another, and do the same.

3. Ask what kind of essay this is–narrative, expository (if so, what kind?), argumentative–and why.

4. Questions of purpose and audience are relevant here and, because "Home and Travel" comes from an autobiography, could lead to substantial consideration of that form.

5. Some time could be well spent examining this essay for patterns of movement between specific examples/episodes and passages of reflection and commentary. You might ask students exactly how these elements function as parts of the whole essay. Does Mead give rhetorical clues to alert the reader to shifts (as in the paragraph that begins "Taken together")?

6. Consider "Home and Travel" as a cultural document. What does it say about role definition for women? About the power of cultural forces?

7. Ask students to characterize the persona of the writer of "Home and Travel."

Suggested Writing Assignments

1. Write an essay about what the word "home" means to you. You might enlarge that by discussing what it means to others, both inside and outside your culture.

2. Compare/contrast Mead's understanding of "home" with that of Joan Didion in "On Going Home" (NR 69, SE 40).

3. Mead was a provocative, often controversial guest on television talk shows, where she frequently aired her views on contemporary culture and behavior. In the middle section of "Home and Travel" (paragraphs 13, 14, 15), she offers some commentary on "children today." Respond to her analysis with an essay of your own.

Additional questions on this essay will be found in the text (SE 63).

BENJAMIN STEIN

Whatever Happened to Small-Town America?

Shorter Edition, p. 64

Benjamin Stein's provocative essay offers a personal view of the American entertainment industry. In the process of attempting to establish two points–that television and movies have presented a negative image of small-town America and that the writers and producers involved are motivated by political factors–Stein develops a cultural critique. He argues that television's consistent depiction of small-town America as "evil and threatening" is not only misleading but patently false. While Stein's sharp wit and effective use of descriptive detail make this an engaging essay, the careful reader should look closely at Stein's assumptions and evidence to evaluate the political context and determine the fairness of Stein's resourceful argument.

Analytical Considerations

1. Ask students to summarize Stein's purpose.
2. Have students comment on the effectiveness of Stein's narrative opening. This may provide an opportunity to talk about a problem many students have in writing essays: crafting an interesting and appropriate introduction.
3. Readers of this essay need to analyze a number of rhetorical elements, including:
    a. Assumptions made (and used) by Stein;
    b. The kinds of support offered by Stein as evidence to buttress his argument; and
    c. The use of repetition and its effects on the reader.
4. Matters of tone and style in this essay are related to a larger question: What are the prejudices of this writer? Though this discussion could become unpleasant, rhetorical considerations require that it take place.

Suggested Writing Assignments

1. Argue against Stein's thesis. Herbert J. Gans's response and Stein's reply provide all that is needed.
2. Write a rhetorical analysis of "Whatever Happened to Small-Town America?" Begin with analysis, and move toward evaluation.
3. Students with significant interest in the subject might want to read portions (or all) of Richard J. Hofstadter's *Anti-Intellectualism in American Life*, then to write an essay about its relevance to Stein's essay.
4. Counter Stein's argument with an essay on how cities are depicted on television. Are they not often ridiculed (e.g., Detroit, Buffalo)? Is television just as offensive to cities as to small towns? Explain.

JANE HOWARD

Pomp and Circumstance in Groundhog Hollow

The Norton Reader, p. 134, Shorter Edition, p. 76

Jane Howard's "Pomp and Circumstance in Groundhog Hollow" presents an affecting portrait of working-class life in America. Through her description of spirited, plainspoken Tildy Hastings, mother of twelve, amateur nurse, voracious reader ("a novel a night"), and seamstress, Howard immerses the reader in the world of mining families in the "Coal Bin of America," McDowell County, West Virginia. Howard's informal, journalistic style, her keen eye and ear for the telling details of daily life, and her sympathetic account of the pleasures and hardships of Tildy Hastings's life create a narrative that is engaging and moving.

Analytical Considerations

1. Re: content
   a. What is the title given to McDowell County?
   b. At what grade level did Tildy's formal education end?
   c. Wayne Hastings's giving up alcohol coincided with what event in his life?
   d. Why is it that none of Tildy's children live in West Virginia?
   e. What is Tildy's philosophy of marriage?

2. Describe Tildy Hastings. How did Howard create such a clear picture of Tildy and her life?

3. Why is reading so important to Tildy? What role does the church play in her family life?

4. Is Howard an objective narrator, or does she have a point of view about Groundhog Hollow that is conveyed by her tone and use of detail? Does Howard indicate a point of view about American values or the inequalities of life in America? What is Howard's relationship with her subjects?

5. To what extent does the "outside" world impinge on Groundhog Hollow?

6. Ask students to comment on the title. Is it appropriate? Ironic? Condescending?

Suggested Writing Assignments

1. Write an imaginative narrative describing the important events in the life of one of the Hastings children who left.

2. In some ways it seems that Tildy Hastings lives in a time gone by, untouched by, perhaps even unaware of, recent social and political changes in the lives of American women. Write an essay on your view of Tildy's status as an American woman. Is she "self-fulfilled"? Is hers a marriage of "equal partners"? Do these terms pertain to her life?

3. Does Tildy Hastings represent ideas, attitudes, and accomplishments that are important aspects of what we think of as life in America? Does she have a symbolic role of sorts?

VIRGINIA WOOLF

My Father: Leslie Stephen

The Norton Reader, p. 146; Shorter Edition, p. 83

Virginia Woolf, one of the finest novelists and most sensitive literary critics of the twentieth century, was also an acute reader and renderer of character. She is able in this portrait of her father, a great thinker and writer in his own right, to bring the man to life. But we are certainly (and perhaps naturally) given a biased view of Stephen. Try as she might to leaven her praise with honest evaluation, the loving and admiring daughter creates a flowing portrait, a picture of a paragon of men. Leslie Stephen perhaps was a paragon, a model scholar, father, and friend, but most readers will want further confirmation, something more than Virginia Woolf's lovely testimonial.

Analytical Considerations

1. While the ostensible subject of this piece is Leslie Stephen, you might lead students to uncover another "subject" here: Virginia Woolf herself. Begin perhaps by asking, "Who is the subject of this essay?" This is a productive exercise, for it can lead to a discovery that the writer can also consciously or unconsciously be a subject of her own writing.

2. Examine the text of the essay for clues to Woolf's purpose in writing "My Father: Leslie Stephen." Direct attention to the original context of the essay–that of Woolf's, the devoted daughter, writing her recollections for a general readership (Stephen died in 1904, so this essay first appeared twenty-eight years after his death).

3. We know the audience for the original publication of this essay consisted of readers of the *Times* of London on November 28, 1932. Again, prod students to look for textual clues to open up the understanding of audience, e.g., "Even today there may be parents . . ." (paragraph 10). Finally, you might raise the idea that Woolf was ultimately writing for herself as a means of understanding her relationship with her father.

4. Examine the design of the essay. Does it use time as an ordering mechanism? Does it organize details around abstract qualities that are taken up one by one? Study and label what each paragraph does in the development of the essay.

5. Every good description coalesces about a dominant impression. Discuss the dominant impression Woolf creates about her father. How does Woolf create that impression? Ask students to be specific about assertions and kinds of support (anecdote, quotation, memory, etc.). Distinguish between the use and value of fairly "objective" information (the testimony of others; Stephen's

remarks) and the use and value of fairly "subjective" material (Woolf's own memories and opinions).

6. Let students describe the persona that emerges from "My Father: Leslie Stephen." Walker Gibson, *Persona: A Style Study for Readers and Writers* (New York: Random House, 1969), is an invaluable resource for this work. Students could benefit from a one-page summary with examples from Gibson; though he deals exclusively with fiction, his comments apply equally to nonfiction.

7. In paragraph 4, Woolf describes her father's habit of drawing beasts on the flyleaves of his books and scribbling pungent analyses in the margins; then she notes that these "brief comments" were the "germ of the more temperate statements of his essays. . . ." This aptly illustrates the process of composition for many of us. Students ought to understand that reading offers possibilities for establishing a dialogue between writer and reader, that careful reading involves annotation. You might devote some class discussion to fostering this sense of involvement with the text.

8. Woolf reveals, perhaps unconsciously, some rather unpleasant and dislikable aspects of her father here. Do such elements belong in a biographical sketch? From what you have read do you believe that Leslie Stephen was the "most lovable of men"?

9. When Woolf says of Leslie Stephen, "The things that he did not say were always there in the background" and "Too much, perhaps, has been said of his silence . . ." she directs our attention to an oft-neglected dimension of the text: silences and absences. Ask students to reconstruct the image of Leslie Stephen based on the information Woolf leaves out of her essay. Woolf says of her father that "when he described a person . . . he would convey exactly what he thought of him in two or three words." Let students try this exercise on Woolf, on Stephen, on a fellow student.

Suggested Writing Assignments

1. Have students write a character sketch of a parent or grandparent. Strive for the concreteness and balance that Woolf has worked toward in "My Father: Leslie Stephen."

2. Read two or three other biographical sketches by Woolf. Compare and contrast them on points of subject, purpose, audience, tone, and persona.

3. Read Doris Lessing's portrait titled "My Father" (NR 151, SE 88). Is Virginia Woolf better or less able to render an objective picture of her father than Lessing is of hers? If one author is more objective than another, what accounts for that ability? Is it approach or personality? Write an essay of comparison and contrast of these two selections.

4. How does Woolf define "fatherhood" in her essay? Using examples from "My Father: Leslie Stephen," write an essay on Woolf's conception of fatherhood.

5. Write an essay analyzing "My Father: Leslie Stephen" in light of the principles Woolf herself sets forth in "The New Biography" (NR 738, SE 420).

Additional questions on this essay will be found in the text (NR 150, SE 87).

DORIS LESSING

My Father

The Norton Reader, p. 151; Shorter Edition, p. 88

Doris Lessing's "My Father" should be compared with Virginia Woolf's "My Father: Leslie Stephen" (NR 146, SE 83) as a character sketch, with the goal of seeing differences in approach. Such a study should be of special interest because of the similarities of the authors. Both Lessing and Woolf are modern novelists (Lessing is contemporary), and both are daughters of British fathers who had unusual adventures outside England. Both authors seem to wish to render true portraits of their fathers: Woolf points out peccadilloes as well as gemlike qualities in Leslie Stephen; Lessing begins by announcing the difficult task she is undertaking of writing a "true" account of Alfred Cook.

Doris Lessing's attempt to write a "true" description of her father results in a maturely and sensitively executed character portrait. Lessing is thorough and successful in her efforts to describe her father objectively: She looks into records, considers the views of others who knew him, quotes statements made by her father, and accepts the responsibility of critically evaluating him. However, complete objectivity and definition are impossible, first, because the author's close personal relation to her subject makes her necessarily somewhat subjective, and second, because a human being can never by wholly delineated. One suspects, though, that such limitations finally enrich the essay, for they make Lessing's character portrait all the more human.

Analytical Considerations

1. The essay opens with a rather striking simile, "We use our parents like recurring dreams. . . ." Scrutinize the text for recurrences of the word "dream" and for the presence of related

words like "nightmare." How does repetition work both rhetorically and thematically? Might this essay be called a "dream sequence"?

2. Direct attention to a consideration of the principles of development in the essay. Lessing builds her essay using particular blocks of material. Focus on her use of specific devices–e.g., photographs, quotations, anecdotes, memories–and determine what they contribute to the whole. Consider the architectural design of the whole essay.

3. Re: voice. In the opening paragraph Lessing begins with the first-person plural pronoun, "we," then shifts to three uses of the first-person singular pronoun ("me," "I," "my"). This observation can open up more than a discussion of how this paragraph functions. It reveals an integral element of Lessing's rhetorical strategy: her attempt to establish a shared purpose and identity with her readers. Is she successful in drawing the reader into the process of this essay? For whom is she writing?

4. Is there a single dominant impression Lessing wishes to create about her father? Where in the text is she most effective in trying to create that impression?

5. It is important to have students appreciate not only how but why Lessing attempts to give the impression of objectivity here. What "distancing techniques" does she use? Students ought to notice how, for example, in paragraph 22, the narrator "unobtrusively" shifts emphasis from the objective to the subjective. At least in certain areas, Lessing strikes a stance of objectivity. In the end one of the things students must determine is just how objective Lessing is and whether or not complete objectivity is possible, or desirable, in an essay like this.

6. What is the purpose of this essay? Is it a memorial in words? An exorcism? A simple reminiscence? An attempt at definition or self-definition?

7. One of the important aspects of this essay has to do with hiding and revealing. Notice that Lessing tells us her father grew a mustache to hide "a heavily-jutting upper lip"; later (paragraph 8) she speculates that when he changed his handwriting, he may have "created a new personality for himself." While it may be fairly easy to determine what Lessing has consciously revealed in "My Father," it may not be so easy to determine what she has hidden. Nonetheless, it is important to direct attention to absences as well as presences. Ask students what is missing. Discuss whether or not Lessing has unconsciously revealed more than she may have intended.

8. In abridged form this essay was reprinted in *Vogue* (February 15, 1964) under the title "All Seething Underneath." Students might be asked to find the source for that title (paragraph 19), establish its context, and evaluate its appropriateness. Such

discussion gives attention to an often-neglected aspect of an essay: its title.

9. This essay is pervaded by bittersweet nostalgia ("I knew him when his best years were over"). Woolf's essay has something of the same tone ("By the time that his children were growing up, the great days of my father's life were over"). Encourage students to explore both essays to determine how tone is generated and sustained.

10. "My Father" needs to be read as a cultural document, a text through which a certain culture speaks. Prompt students to think about this perspective by asking what the essay reveals about colonialism, racism, sexism, and imperialism.

Suggested Writing Assignments

1. Lessing pays considerable attention to her father's traumatic experience in World War I; she notes that "the best of my father died in that war." Write an essay about what the experience of war has done to someone you know.

2. One of the interesting absences in Lessing's essay is her mother. Of course, she does appear at seven points (paragraphs 3, 20, 21, 24, 26, 28, 33), so she is technically "present," but what is the status of that presence? How much do we learn? Write a biographical essay on Lessing's mother, using just the material culled from "My Father."

3. Read Lessing's essay titled "Impertinent Daughters," written more than twenty years after "My Father." It appeared in *Granta*, no. 14 (Winter 1984). Write an essay comparing/contrasting not only Lessing's attitudes toward her parents but the ways in which she has expressed those attitudes. Can you draw any conclusions about Lessing's development as a person? As an artist?

4. Obtain the text of "All Seething Underneath." Examine it to determine where and how "My Father" was abridged (and by whom). Write an essay in which you consider differences in purpose and audience between these two versions. Which is the more effective essay? Why?

5. Write an essay, clearly based on experience, that illustrates "how a man's [woman's] good qualities can also be his [her] bad ones or, if not bad, a danger to him [her]."

Additional questions on this essay will be found in the text (NR 158, SE 95).

DANIEL MARK EPSTEIN

The Case of Harry Houdini

The Norton Reader, p. 159; Shorter Edition, p. 96

Daniel Mark Epstein's absorbing essay about Harry Houdini, the legendary escape artist and illusionist, portrays Houdini as more than a master showman. It depicts him as a brilliant technician, a gifted athlete, and a courageous individual who time and time again outwitted authority on its own terms. In an attempt to demythologize Houdini, Epstein explains how the magician's precise technical knowledge of all manner of locks enabled him to become a great escape artist. In the process Epstein reveals a man of little-known dimensions: Houdini, born Erich Weiss, was a devout Jew schooled in the rabbinical tradition as well as a serious student of magic and the occult. Yet Epstein acknowledges that all research and investigation have failed to account for some of Houdini's greatest feats. Coupled with Houdini's widow's curious comments in a letter to Sir Arthur Conan Doyle, these inexplicable accomplishments lead Epstein to admit that we confront mystery of some sort when we examine "The Case of Harry Houdini."

Analytical Considerations

1. Re: content
   a. How did Houdini explain his abandoning his trick of making an elephant disappear?
   b. Where did Houdini go first in each country he visited in 1900?
   c. On what charge did Houdini sue Inspector Graff and the Imperial Police of Germany?
   d. What does Epstein offer as a metaphorical interpretation of Houdini's escape act?
   e. Name one of the four great tricks still unexplained.

2. Ask students as part of the reading assignment to write what they know of Houdini before they read "The Case of Harry Houdini." In class, ask them what they have learned from reading the essay.

3. In paragraph 1 Epstein poses two questions. How does he answer them in the course of the essay? Are his answers satisfactory?

4. You may want to give some consideration to the ways by which Epstein achieves a fluent narrative style. His sense of narrative detail, use of transitions, careful pacing, and ability to generate interest are notable.

5. Study paragraph 17, in which Epstein speaks of "Houdini's creation of a theatrical metaphor." Ask if the metaphorical

possibilities of Houdini's career constitute his essential appeal for Epstein. If so, what is the central metaphor?

6. Why does Epstein include the story of Houdini's visit to Wiljalba Frikell? What effect does it have? Does its inclusion have a rhetorical purpose?

7. Have students examine the last paragraph of the essay and describe its function and effect. Does it clarify Epstein's purpose?

Suggested Writing Assignments

1. Epstein's account of Harry Houdini versus the German police suggests that Houdini's miracles extended beyond the boundaries of the stage. What was Houdini's relationship to the German authority? Why did he pose a particular threat? In what ways did Houdini "beat" the authorities?

2. Write a character sketch of Harry Houdini, the individual, the performer, the powerful figure in American mythology. How do you account for his popularity?

3. Research the topic of spiritualism in turn-of-the-century America. Present your idea of the origins and influence of the movement.

Additional questions on this essay will be found in the text (NR 170, SE 107).

MIND

ROBERTSON DAVIES

A Few Kinds of Words for Superstition

Shorter Edition, p. 109

Written for the "My Turn" column of *Newsweek* magazine, this brief, clearly designed essay deals with a topic that fascinates most readers: superstition. Robertson Davies draws upon theological wisdom, a host of examples, and his own experience to argue that superstitious belief is a widespread, if unacknowledged, phenomenon.

Analytical Considerations

1. Re: content
   a. According to Robertson–and theologians–how many forms does superstition take?
   b. What do some peoples of Middle Europe believe happens when a man sneezes?
   c. According to Robertson, where do Orthodox Jews place a charm?
   d. What is the superstition of the gypsy and the Lucky Baby?
   e. Is Robertson superstitious?
2. Ask students to point to, and evaluate, the two methods Robertson uses to develop his essay: defining by example; defining by analysis.
3. Does Robertson believe that superstition has any value? Do students? You might ask them to draw up a list of superstitions they know about for discussion. Ask them to think about the role superstition plays in society.
4. Why does Robertson Davies present examples of superstitions among university professors and students? Is Davies trying to point up an irony or is he trying to show that even in bastions of knowledge the irrational pops up?

Suggested Writing Assignments

1. Using this essay as a model, write a column for *Newsweek* to be called " A Few Unkind Words for Superstition."
2. Explain why "Few people will admit to being superstitious."
3. Do some research and write a short history, with concluding commentary, about several well-known superstitions.
4. Write about one of your own superstitions, relating it to

Davies's point that superstitions may answer some need in individuals who hold them.

Additional questions on this essay will be found in the text (SE 111).

BENJAMIN FRANKLIN

The Convenience of Being "Reasonable"

The Norton Reader, p. 172; Shorter Edition, p. 112

This paragraph is a typical passage from Franklin's writing: witty, controlled, and precisely ordered. But the careful reader should pay attention to what Franklin does with the term "reasonable" in the course of the paragraph. What "seemed very reasonable" in the middle is not by the end.

Analytical Considerations

1. Ask students to describe the persona of the writer. Encourage them to point to elements of the text when responding. What kind of reader did Franklin envision?
2. You might want to discuss the rhetorical mode of this paragraph: Narrative? Exposition? Argument?
3. Direct students' attention to the structure of the paragraph. How does Franklin develop his thought? Does he use transitional devices effectively?
4. In the end is Franklin talking about "being reasonable" or "rationalizing"?

Suggested Writing Assignments

1. Write your own short essay on "The Convenience of Being 'Reasonable.' "
2. Write an argument for or against vegetarianism as a reasonable way of life.
3. Read Carl Sagan's "The Abstractions of Beasts" (NR 180, SE 119), and compare his understanding of human reasoning power with Franklin's.

WILLIAM GOLDING

Thinking as a Hobby

The Norton Reader, p. 173; Shorter Edition, p. 112

William Golding has written an essay of classification analysis, marked distinctively by his own personality. The essay is wrought from a number of wry anecdotes which trace the author's developing understanding of what it means to think from his childhood to his university days. These anecdotes introduce and clarify the three grades of thought Golding seeks to classify, and they also lend interest to his essay.

The essay is unified by Golding's consistently sophisticated tone, characterized by the tension created by an author who obviously finds his past experiences noteworthy yet is detached enough to find the humor in those experiences and to poke fun at himself. It is further unified by Golding's repeated attempts to show how thinking always led him into some sort of trouble, a fact he accepts with philosophical good humor. His repeated references to the headmaster's statuettes frame the essay and demarcate the three classes of thinking Golding posits in the essay.

Analytical Considerations

1. Re: content
   a. Identify the three statuettes on the headmaster's desk.
   b. What is "grade-three thinking"?
   c. What is "grade-two thinking"?
   d. Where did Golding meet an undeniably "grade-one thinker"?
2. Explore how Golding lends unity and symbolic value to his essay by his use of the statuettes.
3. What kind of irony does Golding employ when he describes the hypocrisy of Mr. Houghton and others who told him that he was unable to think?
4. Is Golding's essay of classification written with an ulterior motive? What is the apparent purpose of the essay? What do you think the author's goal is in classifying the grades of thinking as he does?
5. Does Golding exemplify grade-one thinking as fully as he does the two lower grades of thought? Does the section on grade-one thinking make this type of thought sufficiently clear? What function, if any, does the described encounter with Einstein serve in defining grade-one thinking?

Suggested Writing Assignments

1. Write a character description of someone you know who evidences one of the three grades of thinking Golding establishes. Be sure to relate incidents and actions or dialogue which reveal the appropriateness of categorizing the person as you do.
2. Do you think it is possible for anyone to pursue thinking as a hobby or a profession today?
3. Think about individuals past and present whom you would classify as grade-one thinkers. Write an essay about the figure who has most influenced the way we, as individuals and as a society, perceive ourselves and our world.
4. Do you perceive any danger in thinking? Why or why not?

Additional questions on this essay will be found in the text (NR 179, SE 118).

CARL SAGAN

The Abstractions of Beasts

The Norton Reader, p. 180; Shorter Edition, p. 119

The professor of astronomy and space science Carl Sagan has earned a reputation as a controversial and an imaginative thinker whose ideas challenge the anthropocentrism underlying traditional scientific and philosophical thinking. Sagan is perhaps best known as a scientist with solid academic credentials who publicly airs his belief in extraterrestrial life. In this essay, taken from *The Dragons of Eden*, Sagan argues that the distinction humans rely on to set themselves apart from and above other animals–the ability to reason and imagine–is false. He bases his assertion on evidence that at least some beasts, notably primates, seem to have abstracting powers. Though less extensive than in humans, primates' ability to "reason" demands that we reevaluate ourselves and our ethical views. Perhaps threatening, certainly controversial, Sagan's essay is lively and forceful in its skillful interweaving of theory, anecdote, and illustration.

Analytical Considerations

1. Re: content
   a. Who said of animals, "The defect that hinders communication betwixt them and us, why may it not be on our part as well as theirs?"
   b. Who made the first serious study of simian behavior?
   c. True or false: Chimpanzees have swearwords.

d. Basic English corresponds to about how many words?
e. Name one of the chimpanzees taught American sign language.

2. Consider spending some class time on a careful analysis of the introduction. Is there a thesis statement? Does it predict the scope of the essay?

3. You might analyze the ways in which Sagan develops his argument, letting students point out the two distinct parts (one equals paragraphs 3 to 14; two equals paragraphs 15 to ?).

4. Ask students about Sagan's tone. Is he belligerent or provocative? For reasons of conviction or rhetoric?

5. Ask what paragraphs constitute the conclusion. Is it expected? Effective?

6. This is a good essay to teach the technique of the rhetorical question. Ask students to note where they occur (paragraphs 1, 2, 5, 14, 23, 25, 26) and how they function.

7. For whom did Sagan write "The Abstractions of Beasts"?

Suggested Writing Assignments

1. Two abilities--abstract thinking and language use--seem to be the most important factors in intelligence. Define "abstraction" and "langugage," and explain their relationship with each other. Why are these elements crucial in a consideration of the value of species?

2. Write an essay comparing and contrasting the views of Carl Sagan in "The Abstractions of Beasts" and Jacob Bronowski in "The Reach of Imagination" (NR 194, SE 133).

3. Write an essay in response to either of Sagan's questions:
a. "How smart does a chimpanzee have to be before killing constitutes murder?"
b. "What further properties must he [the chimpanzee] show before religious missionaries consider him worthy of attempts at conversion?"

NEIL POSTMAN

Confusing Levels of Abstraction

The Norton Reader, p. 187; Shorter Edition, p. 127

With the aim of helping readers think more clearly and communicate more effectively, Neil Postman here classifies and illustrates the kinds of logical fallacies to which we fall prey. Postman uses Bertrand Russell and Alfred North Whitehead's Theory of Logical Types as a means of classifying types of statements; he then illustrates the types with specific cases, showing how statements of fact are blurred with statements of reaction and how generalizations lead to fear and confusion. Misuse of language and logic, Postman asserts, leads to the "stupid and crazy talk" he is trying to eradicate.

In the second part of his essay Postman defines the mode of thinking (variously called second-order thinking, creative thinking, reframing, lateral thinking) that allows us to step beyond the "frame" of a problem. If we can get beyond our assumptions, we can find the creative solutions to the problems at the root of the "crazy talk."

Analytical Considerations

1. Re: content
   a. Who wrote *Principia Mathematica*?
   b. What does Postman mean by "extensional statements"?
   c. What does Postman mean by "intensional statements"?
   d. The more details we have, the higher or lower is the level of abstraction?
   e. Distinguish between "first-order thinking" and "second-order thinking."

2. Ask students to summarize Postman's thesis. Has he written an explicit thesis statement? If so, is it effectively placed?

3. Have students outline the structure and means of development of "Confusing Levels of Abstraction." What kinds of evidence has Postman used to support his argument? What rhetorical strategies does he employ to make his case? Is he convincing?

4. Discuss Postman's comment that "One of the roots of what may be called prejudice lies somewhere in our confusion over what may be 'true' in a general sense and what may be 'true' in a particular sense."

5. Postman's subject and purpose in writing are clear here, but his audience may not be. Have students determine from Postman's tone and the kinds of examples he uses what audience he has in mind.

Suggested Writing Assignments

1. You are in a managerial role. Write an essay in the form of a memorandum in which you explain the technique of lateral thinking and show how it could be applied to a problem of immediate concern to your reader.

2. Drawing on research, write an essay that illustrates Postman's contention that "statistical language of even the most rudimentary sort leaves out so many details that it is, almost literally, not about anything."

Additional questions on this essay will be found in the text (NR 192, SE 132).

JACOB BRONOWSKI

The Reach of Imagination

The Norton Reader, p. 194; Shorter Edition, p. 133

Jacob Bronowski wrote books on both science and literature (one on the poet William Blake). For nearly thirty years he wrote in behalf of the idea that science and poetry have the same roots, that scientific thinking and poetic thinking are essentially the same processes. For Bronowski, both science and poetry originate in the imagination, and both are fulfilled by being translated into reality or passing the test of experience.

The subject of the essay–the nature, the scope, and ultimately the value of imagination–is a challenging one. The years the author devoted to the study of this subject are reflected in the clarity of his essay; it is Bronowski's procedure that puts his complex assumptions and insights within the reach of his readers. Through the use of concrete example, cemented together by the repetition of essential points, Bronowski builds a definition of imagination that is inspiring in its view of the human mind and its possibilities.

Analytical Considerations

1. Re: content
   a. Walter Hunter's experiments with dogs grew out of whose work?
   b. According to Bronowski, what are the most important images for human beings?
   c. What parts of the human brain govern the sense of the past and future?
   d. Name one poet cited by Bronowski.
   e. Nothing that we imagine can become knowledge until we have translated it into, and backed it, by what?
2. Is there a thesis sentence in the essay? If not, construct one.
3. Trace the definition of imagination through the essay. What method or methods of development predominate in the definition? To what extent does Bronowski define by example?
4. Examine how Bronowski uses repetition as a means of developing his ideas and as a rhetorical strategy to give strength to his essay. Reading passages aloud can be a useful exercise.
5. Characterize the diction and style of this essay. Does Bronowski rely on technical or learned vocabulary? Is his manner of expression conversational or scholarly? Look for examples to support your view.

Suggested Writing Assignments

1. Read Henry David Thoreau's "Observation" (NR 193), and

compare how Thoreau and Bronowski view the relationship of imagination to observation and experimentation.

2. Carl Sagan and Jacob Bronowski take opposing views of imagination (the ability to abstract) as a distinctly "*human* gift." Read Carl Sagan's "The Abstractions of Beasts" (NR 180, SE 119), and write an essay supporting the view you believe is most credible.

3. Some thinkers argue that contemporary civilization has witnessed the death of imagination. Do you agree? Write an essay defending your opinion.

4. As an exercise in the use of biographical reference materials, present a short summary of biographical information for one of the persons merely mentioned or briefly identified by Bronowski in the essay. (An interesting example might be Ella Wheeler Wilcox. Attempt to clarify Bronowski's claim that her verse fails the "test of imagination".)

Additional questions on this essay will be found in the text (NR 201, SE 140).

ISAAC ASIMOV

The Eureka Phenomenon

The Norton Reader, p. 201; Shorter Edition, p. 140

Isaac Asimov has an uncanny ability to establish a quick rapport with his audience through an informal, seemingly effortless style. His method is to use everyday language whenever he can and to recount scientific discoveries and phenomena in narrative form. In this essay it is interesting to note how quite specific factual information is subordinated, rhetorically, to the narrative. For example, in the case about Archimedes we are absorbed in a humorous and suspenseful story at the same time that we receive a lesson in physics and an example of the involuntary thinking process Asimov wishes to define.

Analytical Considerations

1. Re: content
   a. Where and when did Archimedes live?
   b. For Asimov, who had the greatest intellect after Archimedes?
   c. Where did Archimedes have his great flash of intuition?
   d. What enabled Kekule to solve the problem of benzene's structure?
   e. What is the thesis of "The Eureka Phenomenon"?

2. Along with the assignment to read this essay, ask students to be prepared to account for the success with which Asimov writes an essay on a topic many might consider less than exciting. Focus on Asimov's tone and his attitude toward his audience.

3. Since this essay is so readable, it might be a good piece of writing to study for its use of transitional devices. Reread the essay, and mark transitional phrases and paragraphs. Ask students to describe the process of movement from section to section in the essay and its controlling mechanism.

4. How might traditional scientists respond to Asimov's point of view? Would they see it as an oversimplification of a complex process?

Suggested Writing Assignments

1. Write an essay about how Asimov, Bronowski, and Thoreau understand the nature and function of the imagination.

2. Does Asimov make the Eureka phenomenon seem too easy? Does he sufficiently acknowledge the need to prepare for this phenomenon by voluntary thinking? Write an essay on this question in the light of William Golding's discussion of "Thinking as a Hobby" (*NR 173, SE 112*), wherein the work and sacrifice aspect of thinking is clearly indicated.

3. Write an essay of advice for a fellow student afflicted with writer's block. At what stage and in what way could involuntary thinking be a helpful strategy? Speak from personal experience if you can. Shape your essay with your audience in mind.

Additional questions on this essay will be found in the text (NR 211, SE 150).

EDUCATION

JOHN HOLT

How Teachers Make Students Hate Reading

Shorter Edition, p. 151

John Holt's essay, written in clear and simple style, allows for useful study of several rhetorical modes, for it combines the techniques of definition, comparison and contrast, analysis, and argument into a forceful statement. Holt's concerns and goals are more complex than his title indicates–the simple definition of how teachers make children hate reading. His purpose is both to demonstrate how teachers can foster a child's interest in reading and writing and to show how traditional teaching methods put a damper on this. Definition by cause and effect serves as Holt's vehicle to show how a particular teaching method results in a certain attitude in the child. Holt also relies on comparison and contrast–here of teaching methods that succeed and fail–to underscore his point. Analysis of how children can be good readers and writers comes into play, as does argument. Holt wishes to show why children don't like reading and to promote his innovative classroom techniques as a step toward improving the situation.

Analytical Considerations

1. Re: content
   a. Describe the kind of teacher Holt was at the beginning of his career.
   b. What caused him to change?
   c. What was the Composition Derby?
   d. What is a "private paper"?
   e. Name one method Holt proposes for helping students improve their ability to spell words.

2. Ask students to locate and examine the techniques Holt uses in this essay. How does he make them work together? Suggest that paragraphs 3 to 8 constitute a unit worth considering in itself and as it functions in the overall design of "How Teachers Make Students Hate Reading."

3. Ask if Holt overstates his case. Where? From conviction or for rhetorical effect?

4. Does the problem discussed here lie with the objectives and methods for teaching reading or with the attitude and personality of the teacher?

5. What do students think about Holt's advice "Find something,

dive into it, take the good parts, skip the bad parts, get what you can out of it, go on to something else"?

Suggested Writing Assignments

1. Write an argument to support the assertion that whoever teaches a child to read plays the most important role in that child's education. (Or if you believe strongly that someone else plays that role, make that your assignment.)
2. In the life of every student, one or two teachers stand out as particularly influential and memorable. Write an essay about a teacher's impact on your life.
3. Do John Holt's teaching methods foster the "liberal education" Thoreau mentions in his *Journal* (NR 91)? Do you think Holt's methods will produce the sort of person and writer Wayne Booth ("Boring from Within: The Art of the Freshman Essay" [NR 332, SE 220]) seeks to produce?
4. Holt seems to suggest that students learn best when they are self-motivated. Consider writing a persuasive essay on this topic, using your own experience and observations and, perhaps, interviews with other college students to develop the essay.

Additional questions on this essay will be found in the text (SE 159).

BARBARA EHRENREICH

College Today: Tune In, Drop Out, and Take the Cash

The Norton Reader, p. 226; Shorter Edition, p. 161

Barbara Ehrenreich's essay demonstrates that the satirical spirit of Jonathan Swift lives on. Her targets are the high cost of college and the modern-day attitude that study is only as valuable as its payoff in real-world dollars and cents later on. Ehrenreich makes her point through sharp wit and deft writing, staying clear of stridency by ridiculing herself at the same time that she lampoons materialism and selfishness. Whether or not students see themselves in Ehrenreich's essay, they will respond to her persona.

Analytical Considerations

Students may need some introduction to the art of satire in order to appreciate what Ehrenreich tries to do here. A simple way to present the matter would be to say that satire is a literary genre that aims its weapons (e.g., laughter, ridicule) at a butt (some vice or folly or error or attitude) with correction as its purpose. The satirist's art succeeds when he or she correctly assumes that writer and reader have a shared sense of values against which the wrongs of the target can be judged. Of crucial importance is the development of a persona that is knowledgeable, appealing, and witty.

1. Since satire usually aims at correction, what is Ehrenreich's purpose here? What is the butt of her satire?
2. Although there are comic elements in this essay, it is not comedy, for comedy evokes laughter mainly as an end in itself. Satire uses laughter as a means to an end, a weapon against the butt of satire. Where and how does Ehrenreich use humor?
3. Describe the persona that emerges here. Is it appealing? Knowledgeable? Trustworthy?
4. Encourage students to read and evaluate this essay as an argument. On what kind of evidence does Ehrenreich build her case? Is she logical? Convincing?
5. What kind of society does Ehrenreich envision if things continue as she sees them?

Suggested Writing Assignments

1. Write an essay about whether or not this essay is appropriate for the readership of the *New York Times.* Why did Ehrenreich choose to express herself in this way for this context?
2. Write an essay in which you respond to Ehrenreich by setting forth your own reasons for pursuing an undergraduate degree.
3. Write an essay in response to Analytical Consideration 5 above.
4. Choose a worthy target, and write an essay that reveals some folly to be righted. Read Jonathan Swift's "A Modest Proposal" (NR 807, SE 489), and draw on the strategies of satire to give your essay force.

JAMES THURBER

University Days

The Norton Reader, p. 229; Shorter Edition, p. 164

Thurber is familiar as a creator of humorous stories, fables, and cartoons. In this piece he seems to address his reader from the point of view of a bratty, uninterested undergraduate in conflict with half-witted or half-senile professors. Thurber constructs his humorous episodes in the form of cartoonlike sequences, or jokes, complete with punch lines.

The narrator describes his college career at Ohio State in the way most of us would describe the immature pranks or embarrassing situations of high school. This farcical tone prevails throughout, suggesting that Thurber's brand of satire here is essentially harmless, all in fun. The author "draws" his classmates and professors in this same spirit, their expressions slightly exaggerated for comic effect ("eyebrows high in hope," "his great brow furrowed").

Analytical Considerations

1. Re: content
   a. What is the university of the title?
   b. Which three classes occupy most of Thurber's attention here?
   c. How did Thurber pass his gym requirement?
   d. Why was Thurber the only senior still in uniform?
   e. What one course did Thurber not pass?
2. This essay, written in 1933, still strikes students as fresh and funny. What techniques and characteristics give it lasting appeal?
3. Compare Thurber's style in "University Days" to that in "The Rabbits Who Caused All the Trouble" (NR 806, SE 488) or "The Owl Who Was God" (NR 1123). Can you make any generalizations from them about Thurber's sense of humor?
4. Thurber, the cartoonist, is in evidence throughout this selection. Can Thurber's stories and descriptions be said to be cartoonlike? How does each of the following help to accomplish this effect?
   a. The use of dialogue
   b. The construction of paragraphs
   c. The use of descriptive language
   d. The function of the narrator as "foil" or straight man in the comic scenes described

Suggested Writing Assignments

1. This essay was originally written for the *New Yorker*, with its distinctive audience in mind. Read S. J. Perelman's "The Machismo Mystique" (NR 406, SE 287) or Ian Frazier's "Just a Country Boy" (NR 397, SE 272), and write an essay that profiles that audience and draws some conclusions about how these authors shape their writing to appeal to *New Yorker* readers.

3. Write an essay in which you account for the durability of James Thurber's humor in one or more of his essays. Consider his technique and persona as part of your argument.

4. Are your university days anything like the ones Thurber describes? Write your own "University Days" either as you are experiencing them or in the light of hindsight.

Additional questions on this essay will be found in the text (NR 233, SE 168).

WILLIAM ZINSSER

College Pressures

The Norton Reader, p. 234; Shorter Edition, p. 169

Though the kinds of pressure may change through time, the subject of "College Pressures" is always topical. William Zinsser's essay will find avid readers among university students and their teachers. And his essay deserves their attention, for Zinsser delineates some of the most important problems that plagued both groups in the late 1970s and that continue to disturb them through the 1980s and into the 1990s.

The four pressures on college students Zinsser writes about (economic, parental, peer, self-induced) are, of course, inextricably linked to societal pressures and problems. Virtually everyone today feels squeezed economically. Parents naturally want their children to succeed and have always urged them to do so. With the great economic investment that must be made in a college education, such parental urging naturally increases. Our competitive society not only condones the sort of peer pressure Zinsser describes but makes it natural for students to think and act as they do. Students come to feel that there is something virtuous in pressure, so they create more of it in themselves to use on themselves.

In the face of increasing pressure from within, Zinsser urges students to exercise their "right to experiment, to trip and fall, to learn that defeat is as instructive as victory and is not the end of the world." Only in risking failure do students discover they have the power to shape their own future.

Analytical Considerations

1. Re: content
    a. What was Zinsser's position at Yale?
    b. What does Zinsser want for his students?
    c. Into how many categories does Zinsser classify pressures on undergraduates?
    d. What solution does Zinsser offer?
    e. Who is Carlos Hortas?

2. Why do students "want a map–right now–that they can follow unswervingly to career security, financial security, Social Security and, presumably, a prepaid grave"?

3. Zinsser has organized the central part of "College Pressures" by the analytical method of division. He uses paragraph 7 to set up the division of college pressure into four types. He devotes paragraphs 12 and 13 to economic pressure. Paragraphs 14 through 18 discuss parental pressure especially as it is related to economic

pressure. The other two types of pressure–peer and self-induced–are discussed in paragraphs 19 through 24.

Do you find this method of analysis helpful? What are its virtues? What, if any, are its limitations?

4. Is Zinsser arguing for a core curriculum–i.e., a scheme of distribution requirements drawn from across the disciplines and mandatory for all students? How do students feel about the desirability of a core curriculum that would ensure, for example, that engineering students studied some poetry, art, and religion and that English majors took some botany, anthropology, and music?

5. With the paragraph that begins "Ultimately it will be the students' own business," Zinsser shifts to a conclusion; the last three paragraphs of the essay intensify the conclusion. Do students find Zinsser's conclusion persuasive? In considering the effectiveness of the conclusion, analyze Zinsser's rhetorical strategies as well as his ideas.

6. One of the assumptions brought to light in Zinsser's article is that college students are, on the whole, more conservative now than they were ten years ago. (This phenomenon has been noted by most educators in recent years but is little spoken of publicly.) What other important assumptions about college students and about American culture does Zinsser bring to light? Point to the places where he does so, or explain how he illuminates the assumptions.

Suggested Writing Assignments

1. In "College Pressures" William Zinsser describes students of the late 1970s as "a generation that is panicky to succeed." He goes on in paragraph 8 to suggest that these students are more self-centered, more directed, and more conservative than students of the late 1960s. In an essay that is developed with specific details and examples, define your college generation or predict what college students in the 1990s will be like.

2. One of Zinsser's most interesting observations is that American culture does not accept failure (see paragraph 6). Does this refusal to acknowledge or accept failure have something to do with what Anthony Burgess points to in "Is America Falling Apart?" (NR 384, SE 262) when he says that "evil–that great eternal inextirpable entity–had no place in America"? Compare Burgess's descriptions of America with Zinsser's observation.

3. Write an essay on the positive values of failure. Use your own experiences and insights to support your ideas.

4. Midway through his essay Zinsser raises an intriguing question: "Where's the payoff on the humanities?" How would you answer this question? What value, what payoff, may humanities studies have?

After answering this question on your own, read William G. Perry, Jr.'s "Examsmanship and the Liberal Arts: A Study in

Educational Epistemology" (NR 242, SE 177) and Wayne C. Booth's "Is There Any Knowledge That a Man *Must* Have?" (NR 268, SE 196). Do these pieces force you to rethink your answers to the question above? How so?

Additional questions on this essay will be found in the text (NR 240, SE 175).

WILLIAM G. PERRY, JR.

Examsmanship and the Liberal Arts: A Study in Educational Epistemology

The Norton Reader, p. 242; Shorter Edition, p. 177

This urban and erudite discussion, by an academic counselor at Harvard, may challenge the reading skills of beginning college students. Nevertheless, Perry's essay might well be assigned as initial reading in a required composition course, for it suggests not only our expectations for students in such a course but some of the central goals to which universities are committed.

Perry approaches his point–to show the importance of helping students to learn how to think–in a somewhat unconventional and, perhaps for students, surprising way: He emphasizes the educational advantages of the phenomenon known as bull and seeks to resolve the "moral dilemma" that bull presents to students and teachers alike. "Bull" is distinguished from "cow," the mere presentation of facts, since at least on the surface level it seeks to disguise the student's lack of acquaintance with facts. However, precisely because the "bullster" must work without facts, his or her work demonstrates an ability to think independently and an understanding of the "contexts, frames of reference and points of observation which would determine the origin, nature, and meaning of data if one had any." The good bullster, then, is a good thinker, a student capable of *applying* facts and *generating* ideas from them. For this reason Perry sees the ability of the bullster as more conducive to a liberal education–the sort of preparation we need to deal with the problems of our world–than the ability merely to accumulate facts. Of course, both facts and the ability to think (or to manipulate facts) are necessary components of what Perry would call knowledge. Perry's ultimate goal is in line with the goal of a liberal education: a fertile union of bull and cow, for "Such a union is knowledge itself, and it alone can generate new contexts, and new data which can unite in their turn to form new knowledge."

Analytical Considerations

1. Re: content
   a. On what faculty does Perry serve?
   b. What is a *fabliau*?
   c. Who was Mr. Metzger?
   d. State the problem Perry discerns.
   e. State his solution.

2. How does Perry define "bull" and "cow"? Are these definitions made sufficiently clear? Try to explain the terms in your own words.

3. Analyze thoroughly Perry's use of the tale of the "Abominable Mr. Metzger" in the essay's structure. (For example, discuss the "picture frame" effect of opening and closing with references to Mr. Metzger.) Consider especially Perry's use of the story in the establishment of tone and point of view and for clarification and emphasis of certain ideas.

4. The fact that Perry has divided his essay into four parts (an introduction, followed by three numbered sections) suggests that each section, while related to the others, has a distinct, identifiable purpose. Analyze each section, and try to identify Perry's purpose in each. You might look for a thesis statement in each section. In the absence of an explicit thesis, point out the passages which lead you to Perry's purpose.

5. If you find Perry's essay difficult to read, is it because of his language? Explain the meanings of the following words and phrases: "comparative epistemology," "logical positivists," "*fabliau*," "heuristic," "hermaphrodite," "empirical."

6. What changes should be made in the form or content of this essay to tailor it to student readers rather than to colleagues (other teachers and counselors)? What textual evidence is there for assuming this essay was intended primarily for colleagues?

7. If we regard this essay as an argument, what is Perry arguing for? How convincing is his argument? Explain.

8. "Examsmanship and the Liberal Arts" may be usefully compared with the *Norton Reader* selection by Wayne C. Booth "Is There Any Knowledge That a Man *Must* Have?" (NR 268, SE 196).
   a. Are Perry's and Booth's educational goals roughly the same? In what ways?
   b. Do their discussions of "bulls" and "machines/ants," respectively, accomplish similar ends? How so?

9. As he acknowledges the intellectual strength of the bullster, Perry confronts the moral issue that bull raises:
   a. In the light of the essay as a whole, discuss this assertion from paragraph 5: "Too early a moral judgment is precisely what stands between many able students and a liberal education."

b. The student who bulls on an examination is obviously attempting to manipulate his teachers. He may perceive education as a game whose rules he is either trying to play by or subvert. Explain how because of his ability, the bullster may be, as Perry suggests, led "*through* the arts of gamesmanship to a new trust."
c. Has reading Perry's essay eased any guilt you might have had about bulling? Was that Perry's purpose? Explain.

Suggested Writing Assignments

1. Write an essay on your own views of a "liberal education." You may draw ideas from Perry's essay on others in *The Norton Reader.*
2. Evaluate your own performance as a student. Do you see yourself more as a bull or a cow? After reading "Examsmanship and the Liberal Arts," are you more inclined to seek for yourself the fertile union of bull and cow?
3. Is Perry bulling or cowing in his essay? Is he hardhearted? Elitist? Write a critical assessment of "Examsmanship and the Liberal Arts."

Additional questions on this essay will be found in the text (NR 252, SE 187).

LEWIS THOMAS

Humanities and Science

The Norton Reader, p. 253; Shorter Edition, p. 188

Knowledgeable, witty, and enthusiastic, Lewis Thomas writes as a gifted generalist whose audience is any reader interested in his or her world. Thomas is a physician with impressive credentials (former dean of the Yale Medical School, president of the Memorial Sloan-Kettering Center for Cancer Research) and a practiced writer (columnist for the *New England Journal of Medicine*) with interests in biology, medicine, linguistics, and sociology and especially the interaction of these disciplines.

In "Humanities and Science" Thomas, with a characteristic light hand, makes a compelling argument for a new approach to the teaching of science. Pointing to the historically based misconception of science as study mired in numbers about which there is little left to discover, he suggests a new curriculum based on "ignorance." From the start of school students should study the puzzles of life–the unanswered questions about biology, ecology, and so on–in the same way they study the unresolvable themes of literature or questions of philosophy. No liberal arts education should ignore the "queernesses of nature," Thomas argues, for the humanist with an understanding of scientific mystery might just see the unseen.

Analytical Considerations

1. Ask students to locate Thomas's thesis. Does it assert the central point of the essay? Does it predict its direction?
2. What is the great problem Thomas discerns? How does he propose it be solved?
3. Why might this essay be subtitled "A Meditation on Mystery"?
4. Why does Thomas hold scientists themselves "responsible for a general misunderstanding of what they are really up to"?
5. Have students analyze the analogy Thomas draws between Latin and biology.
6. Let students annotate the text to demonstrate the organization and direction Thomas has given to "Humanities and Science."
7. Ask students to describe Thomas's persona and the means by which he creates it.
8. Ask students to discuss the meaning and function of the following excerpts:
   a. ". . . scientists are themselves responsible for a general misunderstanding of what they are really up to."
   b. "The conclusions reached in science are always, when looked at closely, far more provisional and tentative than are most of the assumptions arrived at by our colleagues in the humanities."
   c. "The poetry of Wallace Stevens is crystal-clear alongside the genetic code."
   d. "Science will, in its own time, produce the data and some of the meaning in the data, but never the full meaning."
   e. "And the poets, on whose shoulders the future rests, might, late nights, thinking things over, begin to see some meanings that elude the rest of us."

Comparative Considerations

Because this is Thomas's most recent essay included in *The Norton Reader*, it might well serve as the focus for discussion and writing on his understanding of what science is and its limits and possibilities. Both "On Magic in Medicine" (NR 450, SE 370) and "The Long Habit" (NR 575, SE 348) speak to this issue. It might be useful to think about Thomas as a man of science and of vision and to explore what his "vision" is. How should science fit into the thinking of the educated individual? What misunderstandings and misuses of science does Thomas focus on in his essays? (You might remind students of Thomas's eminence as a medical scientist as a factor in his attitude toward science and the general reader.)

Suggested Writing Assignments

1. Write an essay of analysis and commentary on "Humanities and Science." How has it changed your attitude toward the subject? Would you like to see its principles implemented as part of your undergraduate education?
2. Write an essay in response to Thomas's comment that "Poetry is a moving target."
3. Write an essay in response to any of the excerpts in Analytical Consideration 8 above, or in response to another of your own choice.

Additional questions on this essay will be found in the text (NR 260, SE 195).

WAYNE C. BOOTH

Is There Any Knowledge That a Man *Must* Have?

The Norton Reader, p. 268; Shorter Edition, p. 196

Wayne C. Booth, a professor of English and dean at the University of Chicago and a distinguished figure in the field of composition, here offers a defense of liberal education in a world where survival takes precedence over the development of the best kind of life. Booth's aim is to persuade his listeners (this selection was first given as a speech to an audience of teachers of writing) to accept his view of the purpose of education. Booth begins his argument by examining the question he raises in this title. He then responds to it, first with an analysis of four definitions of the "creature we would educate." Three of the definitions are metaphorical and call up distorted and simply unpleasant versions of human nature when translated from metaphor into recognizable human equivalents. Asserting that humankind cannot be reduced to metaphor without some element of distortion, Booth puts forth his positive definition of a fully human education. His perception of education, one that yields the "knowledge or capacity or power of how to act freely as a man," is in effect an education in critical thinking.

Analytical Considerations

1. Re: content
   a. How many metaphorical models for the human person does Booth present and discuss?
   b. What is the final limitation of any teaching machine?
   c. What is the meaning of the term "liberal" in "liberal education"?

d. Why is it "not enough to learn how to learn"?
e. Name one of the three domains of knowledge Booth establishes.

2. Why does the definition of crucial terms lie at the heart of this essay? What terms does Booth define? What strategies does he use in the defining?

3. Isolate and discuss the various analogies Booth uses to discuss:
a. The workings of the human mind
b. The human social order
c. The educational system

4. Construct the syllogism Booth implies concerning man, animals, and machines. It would look something like:
If (A) man is an animal,
and (B) the mind of an animal operates like a simple machine,
then (C) the mind of man operates like a simple machine.
How does Booth prove this to be a faulty syllogism?

5. Analyze the transitions in this essay. Consider especially paragraphs 6 and 7 (are they wholly transitional or part of the introduction?) and the means by which Booth moves from his definition of the student to be educated back to his concern with knowledge that a man must have.

6. Booth spends a great deal of time dismissing three models of the human person he finds unacceptable; he does not get to the positive, his own sense, until the midpoint. Discuss the rhetorical balance of this essay. Has Booth spent too much time on the negative? How do students feel about his not answering the title question until the last third of the essay. Is it an effective rhetorical strategy?

7. Ask students how they make their choices about what subjects are to be known, what critical activities are to be engaged in, what values are to be acquired. Are such decisions free choices or are they determined by the pressures William Zinsser speaks about in "College Pressures" (NR 234, SE 169)?

8. One point of contention students reading Booth's essay may have is that women are entirely absent from the discussion. Booth's language is firmly grounded in masculine pronouns that represent the whole of humankind. Does this undermine his discussion? How do students propose to answer the question of the title once "Person" has been substituted for "Man"? Does the answer change or grow as a consequence?

9. You might assign a corollary essay such as Adrienne Rich's "What Does a Woman Need to Know?," in *Blood, Bread, and Poetry*, or "Taking Women Students Seriously," in *On Lies, Secrets, and Silence: Selected Prose, 1966-1978.* The combination of Booth's essay and Rich's will provoke lively discussion.

Suggested Writing Assignments

1. Read carefully a general statement of educational aims in your college catalog. Reconstruct the metaphor implied there for the "creature to be educated." Give your reaction.
2. Write an essay on "The Knowledge We Must Have Today" or "Is There Any Knowledge That a Woman *Must* Have?"
3. Write an essay comparing and contrasting Booth's views on education with those of Barbara Ehrenreich, James Thurber, or William G. Perry, Jr.
4. Write a descriptive essay on your own experience of learning how to learn, how to ask critical questions, and how to choose important subjects. To what extent was your learning dependent on your teachers, on society, or on forces within you?

LANGUAGE AND COMMUNICATION

RALPH WALDO EMERSON

The Language of the Street

Shorter Edition, p. 212

Here Ralph Waldo Emerson, one of nineteenth-century America's foremost writers, takes a customary stand on the side of the spontaneous and natural. Though a graduate of Harvard, he asserts his partiality for the "language of the street" rather than the language of the university. This paragraph is an efficient rhetorical exercise, presenting ideas that might be used to consider "The Convenience of Being 'Reasonable' " by Benjamin Franklin (NR 172, SE 112) and "Death of Abraham Lincoln" by Walt Whitman (NR 696, SE 389).

Analytical Considerations

1. Analyze the style of this paragraph. What role does alliteration play? Metaphor?
2. Have students examine the paragraph sentence by sentence and label each according to type, length, and rhythm.
3. What is the "force of the double negative" or of breaking other rules of grammar/usage? What is the power of a "rattling oath"?
4. What are the valuable elements Emerson finds in the "language of the street"? Why do you suppose educated men need lessons from the street in the use of vivid and concise expression?

Suggested Writing Assignments

1. Find a paragraph of stilted formal prose (perhaps in some learned journal or book on social science, literature, or art), and rewrite it in the language of common speech.
2. Read "Good-bye to All T--t!" by Wallace Stegner (SE 213). Would Stegner agree with Emerson about the vitality and value of street language? Explain, in an essay, how different contexts–or different times–might color the two authors' recommendations to their readers about use of street language.

Additional questions on this essay will be found in the text (SE 212).

WALLACE STEGNER

Good-bye to All T--t!

The Shorter Edition, p. 213

Stegner's article, which first appeared in the *Atlantic Monthly* (1965), is written in a crisp, concise style that defies misinterpretation. As a teacher of writing Stegner can deliver his opinions with a strong "ethical appeal," not only as a man of intelligence and wit but as an authority on the subject. His moral standing is established by his frankness and lack of pretension. (He acknowledges his own use of four-letter words.) Such a stance gives integrity to his study of the "sin of false emphasis" and allows a conclusion we trust more than the expected dictum of the do's and don't's of vulgar usage. Instead, as if he has learned along with the reader from his inquiry, Stegner concludes, "So I am not going to say shit before any more ladies. I am going to hunt words that have not lost their sting, and it may be that I shall have to go back to gentility to find them."

The short essay ends with finesse, as Stegner provides an example of skillfully used linguistic emphasis from personal experience. Notable for his style, Stegner covers his topic without wasting or mincing words. His dry wit is appropriate to his subject and equally restrained.

Analytical Considerations

1. Familiarize yourself with the terms "expurgate," "bowdlerize," and "piquant," which are used in the essay. Has Stegner consciously chosen precise words, do you think? Why was it especially important for him to do so?
2. What does Stegner mean by "I have applauded the extinction of those d----d emasculations of Genteel Tradition . . ."?
3. How does Stegner manage to abstain from making any moral judgments about his subject? Relate this open-mindedness to his clarification of the term "frank" as opposed to the term "dirty."
4. How is the "sin of false emphasis" related to "sentimentality," according to the essay?

Suggested Writing Assignments

1. Select three advertisements from newspapers or magazines that strike you as using language effectively or imaginatively to make a point. Write an analysis of what makes them memorable.
2. Read Michael Herr's " 'How Bad Do You Want to Get to Danang?' " (NR 772, SE 405). Do you consider Herr's graphic

depiction of war "vulgar" or "improper" by Stegner's standards? Why or why not?

JOHN LEO

Journalese for the Lay Reader

The Norton Reader, p. 298; Shorter Edition, p. 214

Written by a journalist of many years' experience with major publications (*Commonweal*, *Village Voice, Time*), John Leo's "Journalese for the Lay Reader" raises important issues about language. In demonstrating how journalists use euphemisms, cliches, and misleading shorthand, Leo underscores the deceptive potential of language. "Journalese for the Lay Reader" is concise and clear, filled with examples that may set students to more closely examining what they read and write. Leo uses humor and an occasional ironic twist as he goes about a serious task.

Analytical Considerations

1. Re: content
   a. How does Leo define "journalese"?
   b. What are "mystic nouns"?
   c. "When baseball players of the 1940s and 1950s were fined for the usual excesses with women and booze, the writers faithfully reported that the penalties were for" what?
   d. "One inflexible rule of journalese is that American assassins must have" what?
   e. What is a pundit?

2. Ask students to locate Leo's thesis statement. If they cannot find one, have them construct one. Why has he chosen not to use an explicit thesis statement?

3. We know Leo's subject and audience (readers of *Time* magazine). What is his purpose? How do we know?

4. While it is obvious that Leo develops his essay chiefly by means of example, it may not be easy to detect how he has organized his examples and concerns into a fluent essay. Ask students to point to those elements that transitions provide and that ensure orderly progress. Does Leo's persona play a strategic rhetorical role in this respect?

5. You might have students consider how hyperbole and self-parody (e.g., paragraph 2, "knowing scribes") work here.

6. Consider assigning a good essay on clichés for classroom discussion. Christopher Ricks's "Clichés" in *The State of the Language*, ed. Leonard Michaels and Christopher Ricks (rev. ed.) is useful, or perhaps something from John Simon's *Paradigms Lost*

(1981) would be helpful. The subject can be profitably discussed for its rhetorical and ethical implications.

Suggested Writing Assignments

1. Write an essay about the dangers involved in the widespread use of journalese. How does the writer of journalese see his or her reader? How may journalese affect not only the state of our language but our cultural health?
2. Do some research on this topic. Examine several issues, chosen at random, of one magazine, or compare copies of three major American newspapers. Mark the texts you have selected for "frequency of journalese." Then write an essay in which you describe and comment on what you have found.
3. From the evidence gathered in Suggested Writing Assignment 2 write an essay in which you evaluate Leo's contention in "Journalese for the Lay Reader."

Additional questions on this essay will be found in the text (NR 301, SE 217).

LEWIS THOMAS

Notes on Punctuation

The Norton Reader, p. 322; Shorter Edition, p. 217

"Notes on Punctuation" provides a lighthearted and witty supplemental reading to classwork on punctuation. Thomas's conversational tone and obvious delight in learning give life to the arguably dry topic of punctuation. His "rules" are likely to be remembered longer than any grammar handbook's prescription, for they are simple, personal, and logical.

Analytical Considerations

1. Re: content
   a. Who is Fowler?
   b. What is the difference between the comma, semicolon, and period, on the one hand, and the question mark and exclamation point, on the other?
   c. Give one reason why Thomas considers colons less attractive than semicolons.
   d. What does Thomas consider the "most irritating" mark of punctuation?
   e. What mark of punctuation can destroy the whole poem?

2. In one sentence, summarize Lewis Thomas's sense of the purpose and value of punctuation.

3. Ask students to evaluate Thomas's opening and closing paragraphs. Do they detract from the serious points Thomas makes in many places in the essay? Why or why not?

4. Thomas writes particularly good paragraphs, for they conform to the traditional principles of unity, coherence, and emphasis. Let students analyze paragraph 2 or paragraph 5.

5. Thomas's tone is especially important here. Discuss some places where his wit and personality come through (paragraphs 2, 5, 9, e.g.) and work toward a description of his persona.

6. In the end what makes this an interesting and engaging essay on a rather dull subject?

7. Does Thomas really believe there are "no precise rules about punctuation"?

Comparative Considerations

1. Apply the principles of punctuation set forth by Thomas here to his other three essays in the *Reader.* Analyze each, then write an essay on whether or not he has lived up to his own principles. Do his views on punctuation suggest a more general stance toward his subject and his audience that contributes to his success as an essayist?

2. Explore what poetry means to Thomas here and in "Humanities and Science" (NR 253, SE 188). The essays by Northrop Frye, Carl Gustav Jung and Robert Frost in the "Literature and the Arts" section might contribute to this exploration.

Suggested Writing Assignments

1. Select a favorite essay in *The Norton Reader*, and analyze its author's use of commas, semicolons, and exclamation points according to Thomas's guidelines. Turn your analysis into an essay on punctuation.

2. Test Thomas's principles for punctuation on several poems. Write an essay on your discoveries.

3. Do you agree with Lewis Thomas that "the essential flavor of language . . . is its wonderful ambiguity"? Elaborate on Thomas's point in an essay.

Additional questions on this essay will be found in the text (NR 324, SE 219).

WAYNE C. BOOTH

Boring from Within: The Art of the Freshman Essay

The Norton Reader, p. 332; Shorter Edition, p. 220

Though his focus is on how to teach students to write well, Wayne C. Booth's ultimate objective is to guide students to think for themselves. Booth views his two aims–good writing and cogent thinking–as complementary; only "thinking boys and girls" will write papers which aren't boring, or in other ways frustrating. As he elucidates the problem of boring essays and potential remedies, Booth himself attempts to be not only organized and clear but interesting and controversial.

Analytical Considerations

1. Re: content
   a. What has provoked Booth to write this address?
   b. To whom is he speaking? When?
   c. What teacher first set Wayne Booth to thinking for himself?
   d. Name one work of fiction Booth mentions as a suitable model of "genuine narration."
   e. How does Booth use an anecdote as a unifying device here?

2. How do paragraphs 5 and 6 set up the rest of this essay? Block off the rest of the essay into sections, and be prepared to explain what Booth does in each section and how it functions as a part of the whole essay.

3. Are Booth's attacks on *Time* and *Newsweek* justified? You might cross-reference "Boring from Within" with John Leo's "Journalese for the Lay Reader" (NR 298, SE 214).

4. Extract three principles for good writing from "Boring from Within." Then compare Booth's philosophy of composition with George Orwell's in "Politics and the English Language" (NR 353, SE 241).

5. Point out examples of exaggeration and satiric humor in Booth's essay. Is the tone these elements create geared to Booth's audience and thesis? Explain. In light of some of his comments, would you call Booth an elitist? If so, what statements make him seem that way?

Suggested Writing Assignments

1. Read the op-ed page in the *New York Times* for a week, and select a column that is not boring. Analyze it, and write an essay that explains why and how the writer succeeds, avoiding the pitfalls of being "boring from within."

2. Test the validity and accuracy of Booth's criticism of popular

magazine journalism by reading several issues of *Time* or *Newsweek*, choosing representative articles, and writing an analytical essay.

3. Select and write about a model of "genuine narration, with the sharp observation and penetrating critical judgment that underlies all good story telling. . . ."

4. Booth does not try to soft-pedal his criticism of typical freshman writing. Does this essay offend you as a student? Does it contain a fair assessment of student abilities and productivity? Does it offer ideas that may help you to write better, more interesting essays? In other words, can you apply any of Booth's cures to your writing?

5. Booth seems to believe that there are topics that can personally engage almost any college student. These topics lie in the areas of "social problems." Think of some topics that most college freshman ought to be able to come up with interesting, controversial responses to. (You might do this as a class to make sure that the appeal of the topics is widespread. Then individually write on one of the agreed-upon topics, and finally, compare your essay responses.)

Additional questions on this essay will be found in the text (NR 343, SE 232).

NANCY SOMMERS

Revision Strategies of Student Writers and Experienced Adult Writers

The Norton Reader, p. 344; Shorter Edition, p. 232

Nancy Sommers's essay provides students and teachers with a common understanding of the revision process from which they can together devise strategies that lead to more effective revision. Appearing originally in the *Journal on College Composition and Communication*, Sommers's analysis of her research findings draws on the semiotics and linguistic theory of some complexity (Barthes, Saussure, Culler) but, through the inclusion of writing samples and the use of analogies, remains accessible to students. Students may well see themselves among the freshman writers Sommers cites; they may also come away with a new sense of the concerns that can be brought to revision to make it more productive and satisfying.

Analytical Considerations

1. Re: content
   a. What was the goal of Sommers's three years' research?
   b. How did the student writers involved in Sommers's research understand the revision process?

c. How do experienced writers describe their primary objective when writing?
d. What did experienced writers have as a secondary concern?
e. Sommers believes that students fail to develop a sense of writing as ______________.

2. Ask students to condense Sommers's discoveries to a short list of major points.

3. Have students outline the structure of Sommers's report. What formal elements suggest that this is a research document? What rhetorical elements? For whom did Sommers write "Revision Strategies"? Do students believe that it has value for them?

4. Assign Adrienne Rich's "When We Dead Awaken: Writing as Revision" (NR 411). Let class discussion move in the direction of a greater, metaphorical understanding of revision as a cognitive process, of revision as "re-seeing."

Suggested Writing Assignments

1. The essays of several important writers are available in draft form; the drafts show the revision strategies used by the writers. Study the text of a revised essay by William Faulkner or Ernest Hemingway and the final version as well. Drawing on your understanding of revision from Sommers and your teacher, write an essay describing and evaluating the revision process employed by the writer.

2. Follow the same procedure for a paragraph or essay you have written. Keep each draft; then list and analyze the kinds of changes you have made. Finally, write a definition of revision for your own use.

3. Compare/contrast Sommers's philosophy of composition and use of rhetorical strategies with those set forth by George Orwell in "Politics and the English Language" (NR 353, SE 241).

GEORGE ORWELL

Politics and the English Language

The Norton Reader, p. 353; Shorter Edition, p. 241

Here is one of the great essays on language and meaning, from one of the twentieth century's best English prose stylists. Because language is "not an instrument which we shape for our own purposes," Orwell assumes an active stance in seeking to purge the English language of errors, obfuscation, cant, and corruption. He does more than diagnose the illness; he offers a prescription that is eminently practical, though not painless. Implied in the reform of the English language is the reform of political systems, for as far as

Orwell is concerned, corruption in the use of language and corruption in politics are connected.

Analytical Considerations

1. Re: content
   a. What are the three abbreviations Orwell accepts as the only foreign phrases a writer of English needs?
   b. What is the source for the good English that Orwell turns into "modern English of the worst sort"?
   c. What is the sole aim of metaphor?
   d. Give two of Orwell's six rules for reforming English.

2. Ask students to describe Orwell's goals and methods in "Politics and the English Language."

3. Does it seem to students that Orwell loses his way in the first half of this essay, particularly after paragraphs 1 and 2, in which he discusses politics and language? Do they think his deliberate postponement of consideration for the five writing samples an effective device?

4. Ask students to locate and evaluate Orwell's use of transitional elements.

5. Does Orwell believe that problems with the English language can be solved by more careful attention to the rules of grammar and syntax?

6. Ask students to bring in examples of the problems discussed by Orwell and to rewrite at least one passage for consideration in class.

7. Have students find and evaluate some of Orwell's metaphors. Are they fresh and lively? Are they dated or drawn from a cultural context too far removed from those of the students?

8. Ask students to summarize this essay by extracting the six statements that best represent the spirit and intention of the writer.

Suggested Writing Assignments

1. Revise an essay written for this course by following Orwell's six rules.

2. Since this is an election year, politicians will be making countless speeches. Find a speech by a politician; the *New York Times* is a good place to look since it is the newspaper of record. Write an analysis of the speech you have chosen; base your analysis on Orwell's ideas in "Politics and the English Language."

3. Select another essay by Orwell, and analyze it according to his principles and standards.

4. Compare/contrast Orwell's rhetorical principles with those of H. L. Mencken in "Gamalielese" (NR 301).

5. Explain why, as Orwell asserts, "to think clearly is a necessary first step towards political regeneration. . . ." On the basis of what he

says in "Thinking as a Hobby" (NR 173, SE 112) do you think William Golding would concur with Orwell's assertion?

Additional questions on this essay will be found in the text (NR 363, SE 252).

AN ALBUM OF STYLES

INTRODUCTION

What is style? The question defies an easy answer, especially if we accept Robert Frost's pronouncement that "the style is the man." But in the same way that we can gain insight into an individual's character by considering his or her actions, we can work toward an understanding of style by examining the elements that underlie it. First define the person, then you have it! Let us say that a writer's style is that personal, recognizable, and inseparable sense of the writer's self that permeates a text. It is the voice the reader hears–clear, distinct, and individual–the voiceprint of the writer that emerges from sustained practice and successive drafts in writing as well as from life experience. It is not superfluous ornamentation or decorative afterthought.

We can speak of different types of prose style, Renaissance or Augustan or baroque or plain style, for example, and isolate telling characteristics of each. At different times writers have subscribed to particular models of style, imitating qualities of sentence structure, word choice and usage, and tone. Jonathan Swift's dictum that "proper words, in proper places, make the style" is perhaps simplistic, yet it is on target, for it is on this most basic level, the level of words, that style is built.

When we ask our students to talk about style, we need to give them some basic questions and considerations to ponder. Here are a number of suggestions that may be of some help:

1. Describe the persona of the writer.
2. What kinds of words does the writer use? From what sources?
3. What types of sentences does the writer create?
4. What kinds of sentence patterns does the writer establish?
5. Do the sentences have rhythm and balance? Is alliteration an important element? Is assonance? How are such effects achieved?
6. Do repetition, variation, and contrast contribute to the prose?
7. Notice how the writer punctuates the prose.
8. Are there significant pauses in the text? How does the writer incorporate both pauses and silence?

You will want to add other considerations. You might also encourage students to develop a handlist for style. The important concern is that students begin to find ways to recognize and discuss the elements of style, for reading, discussing, and writing about selections of noteworthy style can help students develop their own style. The classical tradition of having students imitate models of style can be helpful so long as students are disabused of the notion that they must write that way all the time. Emphasize to your students that all these efforts are directed toward discovering their own styles. Acquiring style can be a slow process, but students can take some comfort in the words of Samuel Johnson on the subject: "What is written without effort is in general read without pleasure."

FRANCIS BACON

Of Revenge

The Norton Reader, p. 365; Shorter Edition, p. 253

Francis Bacon represents the English Renaissance style best termed "sententious," from the Latin *sententia* meaning "a saying" or "maxim." Derived from classical models, this style is formal with development achieved by metaphor and parallel constructions. This passage should be read aloud to give full attention to how rhythm and balance work.

1. What kinds of sentences does Bacon create? Why?
2. What is the effect created by Bacon's references?
3. Characterize Bacon's word choice. What makes it seem "formal" to us? Would it have been in his day?
4. How does Bacon's use of punctuation differ from ours? Is it merely idiosyncratic, or does it mark a different sense of sentence construction?
5. Does this seem like just one paragraph to students?

JOHN DONNE

Men Are Sleeping Prisoners

The Norton Reader, p. 366; Shorter Edition, p. 254

This is a good selection to teach in conjunction with Northrop Frye's "The Motive for Metaphor" (NR 997, SE 616) since it is an extended metaphor or conceit skillfully used for homiletic purposes.

1. How do we know that Francis Bacon and Donne studied similar, if not identical, rhetorical traditions?
2. How does Donne use repetition and contrast?
3. Trace the development of metaphor in "Men Are Sleeping Prisoners."
4. What is the effect of the rhetorical question at the end?
5. Compare "Men Are Sleeping Prisoners" with Paul Tillich's "The Riddle of Inequality" (NR 1147, SE 689).

ABRAHAM LINCOLN

The Gettysburg Address

The Norton Reader, p. 369; Shorter Edition, p. 255

As legend has it, Abraham Lincoln's brief, moving address was scribbled on the back of an envelope. In fact, Lincoln's "Gettysburg Address," the result of considerable revision, transcends time and place as it illustrates the principles of clarity, economy, and elegance.

1. How many sentences has Lincoln written? Are they varied in type and length? Ask students to evaluate the last sentence.
2. Does Lincoln's speech show any traces of the classical rhetoric of Francis Bacon and John Donne?
3. Consider the impact that Lincoln achieves by repetition, not just of words but of constructions like prepositional phrases.

ANONYMOUS

No Dawn to the East

The Norton Reader, p. 372; Shorter Edition, p. 255

This is an interesting passage for study since it belongs to the oral traditions of Native American culture. It serves to underscore an important point pertaining to style: Style is not limited to the written literature of the Western European, for this anonymous Native American speaks in a fluent, moving, and distinctive voice.

1. Can students hear a voice in "No Dawn to the East"? Let them describe it.
2. How does the speaker organize his remarks? Is there a dramatic edge to the narrative?
3. Is there any way to determine whether the speaker is a man or a woman?
4. Consider how pronouns function here. Is there a discernible pattern to pronoun usage? What are its effects?

ERNEST HEMINGWAY

From *A Farewell to Arms*

The Norton Reader, p. 373; Shorter Edition, p. 256

Ernest Hemingway's style is one of the most easily recognized in English prose, and this is typical Hemingway: crisp, conversational, dominated by nouns and articles, filled with words of Anglo-Saxon derivation, free of Latinate influence, and developed by accumulation.

1. How does Hemingway use the conjunction "and" here?
2. What kinds of words form Hemingway's writing vocabulary?
3. Are rhythm, balance, and parallel construction important to Hemingway?
4. What kind of relationship between writer and reader does Hemingway attempt to establish by his prose?
5. Characterize Hemingway's style.

VIRGINIA WOOLF

What the Novelist Gives Us

The Norton Reader, p. 373; Shorter Edition, p. 257

Here, in an essay from *The Second Common Reader*, Virginia Woolf provides her reader with advice on how to read a book. Woolf's style is rather informal, certainly conversational, yet distinguished by easy reference to a range of works only a well-read reader could appreciate.

Analytical Considerations

1. "What the Novelist Gives Us" seems to be loose and discursive. Is the style of the piece at odds with its content? Or is it a rhetorical pose to establish rapport with the reader?
2. Ask students to give a one-sentence summary of Woolf's advice here. What do they think of it?
3. What is the function of reference to Daniel Defoe, Jane Austen, and Thomas Hardy in "What the Novelist Gives Us"?
4. What does Woolf mean by the "dangers and difficulties of words"? Would Eudora Welty ("One Writer's Beginnings" [NR 976, SE 600]) and Dylan Thomas ("Memories of Christmas" [NR 1, SE 1]) agree?
5. Does Woolf use a thesis statement here? Where?
6. Ask students how Woolf has organized her essay. Why, e.g., does she not describe "what the novelist gives us" until the last sentence?
7. What is the most appropriate audience for this essay? Why?

Suggested Writing Assignments

1. Write an essay about what you expect books to give you.
2. Using several examples as illustration, write an essay about how to read a novel.

E. B. WHITE

Progress and Change

The Norton Reader, p. 375; Shorter Edition, p. 258

Written fifty years ago, "Progress and Change" retains its communicative power because of E. B. White's insight into human beings and his ability to craft clear, hard-edged prose. This one-paragraph informal essay compresses sharp observation into forceful expression and invites comparison with Henry David Thoreau (for content) and Benjamin Franklin (for style).

Analytical Considerations

1. Ask students to analyze the first sentence as a rhetorical strategy.
2. Ask students what White's purpose is. Are students persuaded by "Progress and Change"? Do they accept White's assertion that there is "a dim degeneracy in progress"?
3. This paragraph could be broken into two paragraphs. Ask students where and why. Then let them speculate about why White chose not to do so.
4. Has this essay become dated?
5. Ask students what would be an appropriate context for this essay as a spoken presentation. As a written presentation?

Comparative Considerations

1. All of White's writing is distinguished by his use of concrete, sometimes homely, matter-of-fact details. Some are metaphors, others analogies, but all are important to the texture as well as the content of White's writing. On that basis, compare "Progress and Change" with "Democracy" (NR 833, SE 514).
2. Read and discuss "Once More to the Lake" (NR 79, SE 53) as an essay on "progress and change."

Suggested Writing Assignments

1. Write your own essay on "Progress and Change." Limit yourself to one paragraph, and try writing a 500- to 750-word essay on the subject. Be prepared to discuss the differences between the two, not just in terms of the product but also in terms of the process of composition.
2. Write an essay in response to White's observation that "there is always a subtle danger in life's refinements, a dim degeneracy in progress."

WILLIAM FAULKNER

Nobel Prize Award Speech

The Norton Reader, p. 376; Shorter Edition, p. 259

William Faulkner's speech, written in a ponderous and self-impressed tone, provides a useful opportunity to focus on the difference between style that emerges from within and style that is imposed from without. Have students compare their responses to Faulkner's speech and to the Ernest Hemingway excerpt (NR 373, SE 256).

1. What kinds of words does Faulkner use?
2. Study the structure and patterns of Faulkner's sentences. Read the first paragraph aloud, then discuss its effects, rhythmical and otherwise. Has Faulkner used sentence variation effectively?
3. What is the effect of Faulkner's use of "Our" in "Our tragedy"? What is he trying to do? Is he successful?
4. Characterize the tone of this speech.

JAMES THURBER

A Dog's Eye View of Man

The Norton Reader, p. 378; Shorter Edition, p. 260

This is a neat satirical piece from a masterful humorist. Since humor is one of the salient features of James Thurber's style, it might be wise to ask how he creates and uses humor.

1. Why does Thurber capitalize "Man"?
2. How has Thurber determined his paragraphs?
3. What is the point of "A Dog's Eye View of Man"?
4. How is the style inseparable from the content?

JOHN UPDIKE

Beer Can

The Norton Reader, p. 379; Shorter Edition, p. 261

John Updike's well-known reflection on a beer can is not the lighthearted short piece it seems to be at first reading. Rather, it is an ultimately serious reflection on social and cultural change, cleverly focused on a mundane object. It invites comparison with E. B. White's "Progress and Change" (NR 375, SE 258).

1. Does Updike achieve his specificity by the same means as White?

2. How does Updike involve his reader in this paragraph?

3. How do the opening and closing sentences frame this essay? How do they differ from the intervening sentences? Why?

4. In its style as well as its content is "Beer Can" a cultural document?

Suggested Writing Assignments

1. Write a paragraph or two in deliberate imitation of one writer from this section.

2. Enter any selection from this section into a computer system programmed to revise and improve texts. Compare/contrast the original and new texts. What has been gained? Lost? Write an essay about the experiment in style.

3. Consider all selections in the order presented, and write an essay about the evolution of English prose style from Bacon to Updike.

SIGNS OF THE TIMES

ANTHONY BURGESS

Is America Falling Apart?

The Norton Reader, p. 384; Shorter Edition, p. 262

Anthony Burgess offers an eclectic response to his title question, "Is America Falling Apart?" The essay appears to be very loosely connected. While all the things Burgess discusses bear some relation to his initial question, the reader finds it difficult to anticipate what he will say from paragraph to paragraph or where he will conclude. The movement of the essay is similar to that found in stream of consciousness writing; the discussion of one idea often leads Burgess on to another, whose value may only be topical: "The American Constitution is out of date. Republics tend to corruption. Canada and Australia have their own problems, but they are happier countries than America." Yet it is possible to see a purpose in Burgess's procedure. The eclectic nature of his essay and the sense of the unexpected about it appear to complement his view of America.

For the most part Burgess is critical: Ideologically, Americans are impractical and sophomoric; in behavior, they are voracious consumers and unthinking wasters. A component of the neurosis of Americans is that they often take criticism negatively; they fear it because they define it exclusively as a cutting down. They forget that its impulse may be a genial one and that criticism may lead to betterment because it can clarify areas where problems exist. Burgess sees much potential in America as well as much to criticize. America is a young country, but it is also a growing, dynamic country. Americans are by and large naïve, but they are becoming aware of their sins. Like an adolescent, the country is unstable, but from instability can come progress.

Analytical Considerations

1. Re: content
   a. Where did Burgess spend his year in America?
   b. What is Burgess's complaint about the school system where his six-year-old son attended first grade?
   c. What experience brought Americans to the realization that they're subject to original sin?
   d. For Burgess, what is the most directly human of the arts?
   e. What is Burgess's conclusion?

2. What makes this such an engaging essay? The tone? The persona? The content? The structure?

3. How do students react to an outsider criticizing the United States? Does his detachment sharpen his critical powers?

4. This essay provides some opportunities for illustrating the rhetorical technique of hyperbole; a number of passages students are likely to question, indeed should question (e.g., calling the presidency an absolute monarchy), focus attention on the technique.

5. Ask students to cite some valid criticisms made by Burgess in this essay.

6. Examine Burgess's essay for examples of irony. Is the irony more often implicit or explicit?

7. Is the conclusion a surprise?

8. More clearly than some other essays in the *Reader*, "Is America Falling Apart?" is a cultural document. In its range of references, view of the world, and perhaps even attitudes, this essay speaks of a particular place and time. Students should see that and should question whether or not it has mere historical value or more lasting significance.

Suggested Writing Assignments

1. Write an essay of your own on the question "Is America Falling Apart?"

2. Write an essay based on Burgess's remark that "there is more to education than the segmental equipping of the mind."

3. If you have traveled to a foreign country, that experience may have affected your perceptions about America. Write about some of the effects of travel or residence in a foreign country on your understanding of the United States.

4. Read the two versions of "The Declaration of Independence" provided in *The Norton Reader* (NR 824, 828, SE 506, 510). Do these documents seem the mistake that Burgess claims they are? Note that Burgess calls America "a revolutionary republic based on a romantic view of human nature," that he refers to the "dangerous naiveté" of "The Declaration of Independence," and that he insists, "The American Constitution is out of date." Respond to these charges in writing.

Additional questions on this essay will be found in the text (NR 390, SE 268).

PHYLLIS ROSE

Shopping and Other Spiritual Adventures

The Norton Reader, p. 394; Shorter Edition, p. 269

"Shopping and Other Spiritual Adventures" is a brief, clear, and precise essay on one of contemporary America's most popular activities, shopping. Indeed, shopping may be outranked only by sex and sports. Rose describes the essentials of this activity at three different locations in Middletown, Connecticut (Waldbaum's Food Mart, Caldor, and Bob's Surplus). Her sharp powers of observation and reflection on what she has observed make this an interesting piece about something very easily ridiculed or satirized. Rose's sense of herself as an ordinary person–at play in the fields of Waldbaum's in February, bored on a midwinter Sunday afternoon, or looking for that all-American uniform a pair of blue jeans–gives "Shopping and Other Spiritual Adventures" considerable appeal.

Analytical Considerations

1. Re: content
   a. Where does Rose live?
   b. Why does Rose go to the Caldor store?
   c. What is the purest form of shopping?
   d. What does Rose give as an example of "a kind of shopping in which the object is all-important"?
   e. What does Rose mean by the "spiritual side" of shopping?

2. Ask students to list what Rose calls the purposes of shopping. Would they add any of their own?

3. What distinction does Rose make between buying and shopping?

4. Why does Rose write about shopping for a pair of blue jeans?

5. How would students characterize the persona of the writer here?

6. Ask students to outline the structure of "Shopping and Other Spiritual Adventures"; ask that they indicate patterns of movement in the piece. Is the last sentence her thesis?

Suggested Writing Assignments

1. Write an essay titled "Shopping as a Form of Therapy."

2. Write a description/commentary on an afternoon at a shopping mall.

3. Do you agree with Rose's contention that "We Americans are beyond a simple, possessive materialism"? Respond in an essay that

would be appropriate for the "Hers" (or "His") column of the *New York Times.*

Additional questions on this essay will be found in the text (NR 397, SE 271).

IAN FRAZIER

Just a Country Boy

The Norton Reader, p. 397; Shorter Edition, p. 272

First appearing in the *New Yorker*, "Just a Country Boy" shows Ian Frazier's skill at deftly poking fun at himself as narrator, his audience, and his topic, here, the clichés of country music. Frazier's goodhearted ironic humor animates and lends some coherence to the barrage of quick, interrelated remarks that make up "Just a Country Boy." Because it is arguably more a comic monologue than an essay, students can read Frazier's piece for the rhythm of its humor. They may also see themselves in the audience Frazier spoofs: those yuppies seeking a bit of regional color to relieve the monotony of gray flannel by becoming "country."

Analytical Considerations

1. Ask students to summarize subject, purpose, and audience in one sentence.
2. What is the first textual clue that this is a satire? Ask students to cull other textual clues, then to state the object of Frazier's satire.
3. Ask students if this piece has a thesis statement, a clear beginning? (If not, what is the deliberate design of the opening meant to do?) Does it have a conclusion?
4. Characterize the kind of relationship Frazier establishes between speaker/writer and audience. How does he develop it?
5. Is this an essay? Ask students if it would "work" on "Saturday Night Live."
6. Do students accept as a cultural document Frazier's view of what it means to be "a country boy"–i.e., does he have all the right preferences, attitudes, jargon, and tics in place?

Suggested Writing Assignments

1. Read several other pieces by Frazier, perhaps "Dating your Mom" or "The Museum" from *Dating Your Mom* (1986) or something from *Nobody Better, Better Than Nobody* (1987), his most recent collection. Write an essay in which you give a profile of Frazier as a satirist–say, his characteristic persona(s), his customary

targets, and his standard rhetorical strategies. You might compare/contrast him to another *New Yorker* satirist like Garrison Keillor or S. J. Perelman.

2. Do some research on the history of American country music and its recent increase in popularity. Write an analytical essay in which you attempt to set out the causes and effects of this cultural phenomenon.

JOHN McMURTRY

Kill 'Em! Crush 'Em! Eat 'Em Raw!

The Norton Reader, p. 399; Shorter Edition, p. 274

John McMurtry, a Canadian professor of philosophy, has written an essay about his experiences as a professional football player. McMurtry recounts his love of the game as a youth, when "almost no one gets hurt and it's rugged, open and exciting. . . ." Then, with regulation and institutionalization by adults, the joy of the game dissipated. McMurtry writes a strong personal narrative, drawing upon his own career and using that experience to develop a thought-provoking discussion of the impact of organized "game" violence on society. Though the subject may have become somewhat trite in other hands and though McMurtry has a tendency to generalize, his essay demonstrates candor, reflection, and a refreshing humility. It should elicit good discussion and writing.

Analytical Considerations

1. Re: content
   a. What is the writer's present profession?
   b. To develop his contention, McMurtry offers an analogy between football and ______________.
   c. Name one of the two "jock-loving Americans" cited by McMurtry.
   d. McMurtry was so heavily taped as a college player that he earned what nickname?
   e. The successful football player is a prime candidate for a job in what segment of society?

2. Condense McMurtry's contentions in this essay to one sentence. Does he express his major contention in a thesis statement? If so, locate it.

3. By what means does he develop his thesis? With what kind of evidence does he support his assertions? Are students satisfied with the evidence?

4. Ask students if McMurtry's analogy between football and war convinces them that these are equally violent activities.

5. Is paragraph 12 a diversion? An interruption? An integral part of the essay?
6. Ask students to evaluate this essay. Where and how is it strong? Where and how is it weak?

Suggested Writing Assignments

1. Perhaps you have found yourself in a process similar to the one McMurtry writes about: enjoying a sport as a youngster only to have the fun taken out of it by increasing adult restriction. If so, write an essay about the process and its impact upon you.
2. Write an argument calling for the elimination of a professional sport (e.g., football, hockey, boxing) because of its damage to participants and spectators.
3. Write an essay explaining the positive values of participation in organized sports on the nonprofessional and professional level.
4. Write a reflective essay on why professional sports have become such an important part of life in contemporary society.

Additional questions on this essay will be found in the text (NR 405, SE 279).

HERB GOLDBERG

In Harness: The Male Condition

Shorter Edition, p. 281

Herb Goldberg's essay seeks to call attention to and outline the problem of the liberation of men. Goldberg asserts that men must begin en masse to question their sex role assignments or to rebel against them in the same way that women have in recent decades.

Men have individual feelings and needs but are conditioned to suppress or eradicate them or to express them only in culturally approved ways. The male sexual stereotype that both men and many women apply strictly portrays men as "the heroes, the studs, the providers, the warriors, the empire builders, the fearless ones." But for many men the stereotype of masculinity does not fit, and they assume the role only at considerable cost. Men, then, must discover strategies leading to their own liberation.

Goldberg argues that the women's movement of recent years can offer men little that will be useful in achieving their own liberation. For one thing, women's problems are different; women have clearer targets to shoot at and in some cases can achieve change through legislation, which hardly seems relevant to the male condition. And woman have more options; though there remains significant cultural resistance, they can much more "readily move between the traditional definitions of male or female behavior and roles" than men are permitted to do. It follows, then, that the structure, methods, and objectives of the women's movement are not likely to fit the needs of men's liberation. As for the notion that women's liberation will itself help men escape from their stereotypes, Goldberg dissents: "If there is to be a constructive change for the male he will have to chart his own way, develop his own style and experience his own anxieties, fear, and rage because *this time mommy won't do it*!"

Analytical Considerations

1. Explain Goldberg's title. What metaphor does it create? Is the metaphor carried through the essay? Why is the word "Condition" well chosen?
2. Goldberg begins "In Harness: The Male Condition" with an example that is nearly two pages long. Is this technique of introduction effective? Does it inform as much as it whets interest?
3. How dependent is Goldberg on comparison and contrast between men and women to reveal his thoughts? Is discussing women's sex role problems and "liberation" effective in revealing the situation of men?
4. Evaluate some of the images Goldberg employs. For example, consider the "zombie," the "cardboard Goliath," and the "disguises of privilege." Are these appropriate and convincing images? How are they related to one another?
5. Is Goldberg trying to evoke a mood toward the end of the essay when he quotes from several letters? What feelings in the reader does he succeed in evoking?

Suggested Writing Assignments

1. Write an analytical essay which demonstrates how Goldberg's major point is made by defining by cause or effect. Cite specific instances of Goldberg's defining by cause or effect.
2. Describe what you think a liberated man would be like. Is there any one type of individual he would be?
3. Goldberg points out the crucial irony that men have apparent freedom and power, yet their most important components are locked inside them. Write an essay explaining why you agree or disagree with Goldberg's assessment.

Additional questions on this essay will be found in the text (SE 286).

S. J. PERELMAN

"The Machismo Mystique"

The Norton Reader, p. 406; Shorter Edition, p. 287

S. J. Perelman, resident humorist at the *New Yorker* for many years, satirized the foibles and pretensions of modern American society for decades. Here he takes on the cult of machismo, the exaggerated and self-indulgent pose of masculinity adopted by some men. Blending personal experience and definition by example, Perelman deflates the macho personality, revealing the whole cult as a pointless, often ludicrous charade.

Analytical Considerations

1. Re: content
   a. Summarize the opening scene.
   b. Who is Rick Ferret?
   c. Who is the "holder of the black belt [of machismo] in the Anglo-Saxon world"?
   d. Who was "Papa"?
   e. To whom does Perelman refer as the "little corpuscle"?
2. What is machismo?
3. What is Perelman's purpose here? What audience does he have in mind?
4. Perelman devotes paragraph 19 to a discussion of "literary *machos*." Why? Is this clearly related to his purpose, or has he wandered from the point?
5. How does Perelman use different levels of diction in this essay?
6. Perelman begins his essay with the narrator's saga of his attempts to cultivate a macho image. Ask students to list textual clues which alert the reader to this as a rhetorical pose.
7. In regard to Perelman's craftsmanship, how does he use the opening narrative, with its putdown of "Such *machismo*–who would have expected it from a shrimp like you?" and the closing narrative of Earl Sande? How are they related? Do they both enhance the machismo of the narrator?
8. How does Perelman classify the different types of macho men?

Suggested Writing Assignments

1. Write an essay about the presence of the macho personality in contemporary society. Who is responsible for perpetuating it? Is it valued by both men and women? What are the dangers?
2. Advertising is filled with copy that seeks to create and

propagate the macho mystique. Study several magazines, and gather some advertisements for analysis and commentary.

3. Write a speculative essay in which you explore the reasons why some men might feel it necessary to develop a macho personality.

4. Write an essay comparing/contrasting Perelman with any other satirist in the *Reader* (e.g., Jonathan Swift, Garrison Keillor, James Thurber).

Additional questions on this essay will be found in the text (NR 410, SE 291).

BETTY ROLLIN

Motherhood: Who Needs It?

The Norton Reader, p. 430; Shorter Edition, p. 292

Though it is a relatively short essay, Betty Rollin's "Motherhood: Who Needs It?" is quite complex and will generate a strong response from students who read it with care. In her essay Rollin brings to light and rigorously analyzes many of the assumptions about motherhood. She begins with a brief, direct rejection of the "Motherhood Myth–the idea that having babies is something that all normal women instinctively want and need and will enjoy doing." She then moves to consider the historical roots of the Motherhood Myth, dwelling on its persistence and examining how the myth is perpetuated: "So if the music is lousy, how come everyone's dancing?" Social conditioning is the broad answer. Initiated by parents and fostered by peers, the conditioning leads eventually to women who look to motherhood as a way of avoiding the task of developing themselves.

The last three paragraphs serve to clarify that Rollin is not at all opposed to motherhood: "Only the Myth must go out. . . ." She seeks to limit births in an overpopulated world, and she encourages responsible parenthood for the sake of loved and happy people, including mothers.

Analytical Considerations

1. State the thesis in one sentence.

2. Examine the diction (e.g., "baloney," "rotten," "Freud's magnificent daughter," "beefing up," "got the ball rolling") and other means by which Rollin establishes a persona in this essay. Does she come across as likable? Fair? Honest? Trustworthy? Learned?

3. Draw up a list of ten assertions Rollin makes; scrutinize each for accuracy, then look for the kind of support she uses.

4. Rollin sometimes uses generalizations. Have students evaluate

the evidence she uses to support her assertions. Does she deal with the other side of the issue? How?

5. Examine the assumption of overpopulation. What constitutes overpopulation? Are the horrors of overpopulation overstated? (A number of respected scientists now believe that the problem of starvation is due not to an inability to grow/harvest sufficient food for the world's population but to political factors that prevent distribution of resources.)

6. Explain how Rollin defines by negation in the first few paragraphs of the essay.

Suggested Writing Assignments

1. This essay appeared in 1970. Do you think its concerns are still vital in the late 1980s? Or do you view it as dated in some way? Write an essay about the timeliness of Rollin's assessment.

2. Write your own response to the question "Motherhood: Who Needs It?"

3. Write an essay of illustration based on this statement from "Motherhood: Who Needs It?":" . . . people tend to be sort of good sports about what seems to be inevitable." Choose any issue that makes a compelling illustration of this remark.

4. Rollin's use of myth can be viewed as restrictive. Read Robert Graves's essay "Mythology" (NR 1124), and write an essay about the positive understanding and influence of the myth of motherhood. Consult the *Oxford English Dictionary* to acquire sure senses of "myth" and "mythology."

5. Write an essay on "Fatherhood: Who Needs It?"

JOAN DIDION

Salvador

The Norton Reader, p. 464; Shorter Edition, p. 302

This excerpt from Didion's book of the same title illustrates her distinction as a writer of first-rate descriptive prose. "Salvador" combines narrative interest with journalistic precision and descriptive power so skillfully that the reader feels present at the scene. Didion was criticized by some for spending only two weeks in this strife-torn Central American country. How could she really grasp a sense of what was happening, these critics asked. Reading just this excerpt answers that question. Didion's methodical scrutiny of people, events, landscape, traffic, hotels, even documents yielded information of unusual depth and range. Furthermore, Didion has structured her prose so that the essay develops by an accumulation of images. Each section coalesces about a particular image while juxtaposition and repetition, rather than customary transitional devices, bind "Salvador" together. Total effect is what is important here. In the end the reader both knows and feels what life and death are like in a land where the "mechanism of terror" is the most powerful social force.

Analytical Considerations

1. Re: content
   a. What is an "amnesiac fugue"?
   b. What is the "grim-gram"?
   c. What is the "Puerto del Diablo"?
   d. How long was Didion in El Salvador?
   e. What is the most striking architectural feature of houses in the San Benito and Escalón districts of San Salvador?

2. Ask students to decide the dominant impression Didion wishes to create in "Salvador." How does she go about doing that?

3. Discussion of Analytical Consideration 2 should involve consideration of Didion's descriptive powers; if it does not, direct discussion to her abilities by asking students what "things" stay in mind after reading the piece. They are likely to say something about the dominant impression (terror) and something about particular images, say, a Cherokee Chief or photo of a disfigured corpse, both of which merit discussion. In regard to the disfigured corpse, analyze paragraph 6 in particular. What is Didion doing here? How has she used description to create an image that is emblematic? As for the Cherokee Chief, why does Didion not feel she has to describe this vehicle for her reader? What is its emblematic value?

4. Have students speculate about Didion's purpose and audience. Would this be an appropriate dispatch for publication in a newspaper? Why/why not? Which one?

5. Has Didion made a political statement in "Salvador"?

6. What holds "Salvador" together? Thesis? Structure? Persona? Imagery?

7. How do students reads the ellipses at the end of paragraphs 2 and 18? (They are Didion's, not the editors'.)

Comparative Considerations

1. Joan Didion has said that writing is "the act of saying 'I,' of imposing oneself upon other people, of saying, 'listen to me, see it my way, change your mind.' " Ask students how "Salvador" does/does not illustrate this definition. Why does Didion want others to listen to her? Is it to change their minds? About what? This seems particularly important in regard to "Salvador," but it might well be applied to the other selections by Didion in the *Reader.* What does she want seen her way in "On Going Home" (NR 69, SE 40) or in

"On Keeping a Notebook" (NR 731, SE 414) or in "Georgia O'Keeffe" (NR 1098, SE 673)? You might well encourage students to develop an understanding of Joan Didion's sense of her "vocation" as an artist. That discussion could provide some substantial topics for essays.

2. In "On Keeping a Notebook" Didion says that "the point of my keeping a notebook has never been, nor it is now, to have an accurate factual record of what I have been doing or thinking. That would be a different impulse entirely, an instinct for reality which I sometimes envy but do not possess." Fifteen years later she wrote "Salvador." Does it reveal her having acquired that "instinct for reality"?

Suggested Writing Assignments

1. Write an essay in which you account for the power and impact of Didion's writing in "Salvador."

2. Turn your response to Analytical Consideration 5 into an essay.

3. Write an essay comparing and contrasting, on whatever bases you choose, George Orwell's "Politics and the English Language" (NR 353, SE 241) with Joan Didion's "Salvador."

Additional questions on this essay will be found in the text (NR 471, SE 309).

JONATHAN SCHELL

The Destructive Power of a One-Megaton Bomb on New York City

The Norton Reader, p. 472; Shorter Edition, p. 310

Schell's essay, which originally appeared in the *New Yorker*, is written with care and a near-clinical precision. Its rhetorical strengths are clear: a simple and emphatic thesis that accurately predicts the purpose and scope of the essay; efficient organization with assertions carefully made and supported; a clear sense of audience. For all that, students may indeed ask why is there no conclusion and what is Schell's purpose other than description. Both questions are well worth exploring.

Analytical Considerations

1. Locate and evaluate the thesis for this essay. Divide the essay into its three sections, and determine why it has been divided thus.

2. Why has Schell avoided leading the reader to a particular

conclusion? What does this say about his sense of audience? How do students feel about being "written to" in that way?

3. Does Schell's failure to articulate particular conclusions and judgments mean that he has no point to make?

4. This essay on an emotionally charged topic is noticeably free of emotionalism. Why?

5. Compare the tone in this selection with that of James C. Rettie in " 'But a Watch in the Night': A Scientific Fable" (SE 515). Are both authors objective? Do they handle statistical information similarly? Is one more effective or persuasive than the other? Explain.

Suggested Writing Assignments

1. Garrison Keillor's essay "The Tower Project" (NR 478, SE 319) and Schell's essay were written for the *New Yorker*, as were a number of others included in this reader. If you've not done so, read several of these authors, examine the texts carefully for rhetorical features and strategies, then write an essay titled "the *New Yorker* Reader" or "Who Reads the *New Yorker*?" It might be helpful to review several recent issues of the magazine as well.

2. Conduct a limited survey which investigates the public's familiarity with issues related to nuclear weaponry. Construct your questions carefully. You could focus the survey on the public's knowledge of U.S. and Soviet nuclear capability or on the effects of nuclear warfare. In essay form, make some conclusions about public knowledge based on your evidence.

3. Discuss the psychology of contemporary America as it relates to the threat of nuclear warfare. Do you perceive a mood of hope, resignation, fatalism, or what? How does this mood compare with that prevailing in America during the Cuban missile crisis or the Vietnam War, for example? Can differences be distinguished between the outlook of the present generation of young people who have always lived under a nuclear threat and the attitudes of their parents' generation? Explain.

4. Discuss the argument that nuclear arsenals are "deterrents" to war. Do you agree with those who maintain that they are necessary as a peacekeeping strategy in the present state of affairs, or do you believe that increased energy and research spent perfecting nuclear weapons increase the likelihood that they will someday be used? Explain and support your opinion.

BRENT STAPLES

Black Men and Public Space

The Norton Reader, p. 440; Shorter Edition, p. 315

In this short, tightly controlled essay Brent Staples writes about a discovery he made at the age of twenty-two. Writing about a young woman's flight at his innocent and uninterested approach, he notes that "it was in the echo of that terrified woman's footfalls that I first began to know the unwieldy inheritance I'd come into–the ability to alter public space in ugly ways." "Black Men and Public Space" is an episodic narrative with commentary enlarging upon that declaration. Staples's style is clean, and his skillful use of irony distinguishes the piece, which should give most students (and instructors) something to think about.

Analytical Considerations

1. Re: content
   a. Where did Staples encounter his first victim?
   b. What was her response?
   c. Where did Staples grow up?
   d. In truth, Staples is shy of physical combat. Why?
   e. What tension-reducing measure does Staples employ on his "late-evening constitutionals" in New York City?
2. Ask students to state the problem Staples came to perceive. What was his solution?
3. This is an essay inextricably linked to gender and race; ask students to explain what that means.
4. You might explore two features used in the development of this essay: first, let students determine the four "times" of the piece (childhood in Pennsylvania; graduate school in Chicago; Chicago in the later 1970s and early 1980s; New York City now), and appreciate the way chronology serves Staples; second, have students distinguish between narrative episode and commentary so that they gain an appreciation for the ways Staples has woven the two together in the fabric of his essay.
5. What is the dominant rhetorical mode here: narrative, description, exposition, or argument?
6. This essay is useful for teaching the use of irony; ask students how and where Staples has used irony as a rhetorical strategy. How long does it take to understand that "victim" in the first paragraph is ironic? How is Staples's whistling melodies from Beethoven and Vivaldi the ultimate irony?
7. Ask students how Staples has used two of the great themes of

literature–appearance/reality and the reversal of expectations–in "Black Men and Public Space."

Suggested Writing Assignments

1. Write an essay about what you have learned from reading and discussing "Black Men and Public Space."
2. Write an essay about that "vast, unnerving gulf" that lies "between nighttime pedestrians."
3. "Public space" and "personal space" are terms coined within the last decade. What do they say about contemporary society?

Additional questions on this essay will be found in the text (NR 443, SE 318).

GARRISON KEILLOR

The Tower Project

The Norton Reader, p. 478; Shorter Edition, p. 319

This succinct essay by a well-known humorist and radio personality will provide substantial opportunities to talk about voice, irony, parody, and lampoon. As a master of satire Keillor takes his place in a long tradition that includes H. L. Mencken, Russell Baker, and Woody Allen. Students should develop a working vocabulary of the terms mentioned above in order to appreciate "The Tower Project." Because this piece is compact and efficient, it will be particularly useful in demonstrating the contemporary satirist's art. Keillor has not singled out individuals here; rather, he lampoons the mentality of government and business which endorses what's biggest and newest and seems to one-up the other guy, at whatever cost.

Analytical Considerations

1. Ostensibly this is a corporate or government memorandum. Bring in examples of the form, and test the accuracy and validity of Keillor's essay.
2. Is "The Tower Project" meant to be humorous? On what level? Is humor Keillor's ultimate goal?
3. At what point do we first know that this is not to be taken at face value? List all textual clues that alert the reader to that fact in the rest of the essay.
4. The kind of writing that Keillor attacks here is symptomatic of particular attitudes and patterns of behavior. Why?
5. Ask students to state in one sentence what Keillor lampoons.
6. Ask students who ought to read this essay. Why?

Suggested Writing Assignments

1. Compare/contrast Keillor with Jonathan Swift ("A Modest Proposal" [NR 807, SE 489]) as satirists. Think about such basic considerations as subject, purpose, and audience before you think about more sophisticated rhetorical elements.
2. Write an essay on why people resort to the kind of writing Keillor parodies. What are some of the consequences of its use in late-twentieth-century society?
3. Write a parody of a government memorandum or a letter you've received from a corporation or utility or the dean's letter to your parents about a poor semester's performance.
4. Read George Orwell's "Politics and the English Language" (NR 353, SE 241). How do you think Garrison Keillor would view Orwell's essay?

Additional questions on this essay will be found in the text (NR 479, SE 320).

HUMAN NATURE

ROBERT FINCH

Very Like a Whale

The Norton Reader, p. 521; Shorter Edition, p. 322

The presence of a beached whale on Corporation Beach in Dennis, Massachusetts, prompted Robert Finch to write this essay. This "magnitude of flesh," at first an object of respectful curiosity, became far more than that to Finch, for it led him to pose serious questions, not about whales but about human beings. In the course of "Very Like a Whale," Finch attempts to answer several questions: Why did people come to see it? What were they looking at? What was it that they saw? In this essay about perspective, when Finch takes exception to the anthropocentric view of the whale and later expands the discussion to include all nature, he teaches us something about our own limitations, our relationship with the natural world.

Analytical Considerations

1. Re: content
   a. On what beach had the whale washed ashore?
   b. What kind of whale was it?
   c. What does "anthropocentric" mean?
   d. Why do whales have an inalienable right to exist?
   e. Why did the whale die?
2. How does Finch answer the question of why people flocked to see the whale. What do students think about his answer?
3. In paragraph 1 Finch writes: ". . . thousands of us streamed over the sand to gaze and look." What is the difference between "gazing" and "looking"? What does Finch do?
4. What does Finch mean by calling the whale carcass "an intoxicating, if strong, medicine that might literally bring us to our senses"?
5. Consider devoting some attention to paragraph 7, which is about language, specifically about metaphors and similes. Ask students to evaluate the metaphors and similes applied to the whale in this paragraph. If they work, why do they work? Then ask them to note other places where Finch uses those figures of speech (e.g., paragraph 9). Lead the discussion toward a consideration of when and why we use figurative language.
6. Paragraph 8 can offer some insight into the process of definition. Ask students to list the definitions, then to use the first

two questions which open the paragraph as ways of classifying the definitions.

Suggested Writing Assignments

1. Select a key assertion from this essay (e.g., "our growth as a species depends equally upon our establishing a vital and generative relationship with what surrounds us") and use it as the focus for an essay of your own. Draw on personal experience to enrich the essay.
2. In the Foreword to the book of essays from which "Very Like a Whale" comes, Robert Finch offers some observations that could serve as a departure point for an essay:

> Not only the Cape, but every locale, needs to be measured by the human foot and eye as well as with population graphs and water studies. It needs to be sounded, not merely for its capacity to support human traffic and commerce, but for its seasonal mysteries and secret running life. It needs to be known, not only from soil samples and by planning boards, but in its many moods and expressions, its comings and goings, its various lives and forces that can excite wonder and awe and new ways of seeing. And it needs to be supplied, not just with tourists and oil, but with a love that inspires discipline and commitment from all who use it.

3. Read some of Henry David Thoreau's writing on Cape Cod; then read several more essays by Finch. You might try his latest book, *Outlands.* Write an essay on both writers as observers of the natural world.

Additional questions on this essay will be found in the text (NR 526, SE 326).

BARBARA GARSON

Whistle While You Work

The Norton Reader, p. 518; Shorter Edition, p. 327

Barbara Garson writes about a near-universal fact of life: work. Based upon interviews with a number of people employed at different businesses but doing the same kind of work, "Whistle While You Work" offers some unexpected as well as some expected conclusions. Garson's use of the interview technique gives the essay vitality, narrative interest, and a substantial realism. Clearly, this is an introduction for a text that will develop the seeds of narratives presented here; nonetheless, "Whistle While You Work" has an integrity of its own.

Analytical Considerations

1. Re: content
   a. Who is Starlein?
   b. How did the Haitian box assembler at the Ping-Pong factory amuse himself?
   c. What is the most common motive for assembly-line workers' letting pieces pile up?
   d. What was the most dramatic discovery Garson made?
   e. What was Ellen's dilemma?

2. Ask students to describe the design of Garson's project, then the methods, then the results. Has her essay been structured according to the same three-part scheme: design, method, results?

3. Have students block the essay into sections. How has Garson separated narrative from commentary?

4. What is the effect of Garson's use of conversation and quotation in "Whistle While You Work"? What has her use of the interview technique given to the essay?

5. What does Garson mean by the term "real work" when she writes, "The crime of modern industry is not forcing us to work, but denying us real work"?

Suggested Writing Assignments

1. Write an essay about what you have learned about yourself, others, and the nature of work from your own job experience. In what ways does Garson's essay echo your own experience?

2. Interview several people about their work, and write an essay based on the results. Set your goals, and design a questionnaire beforehand.

DESMOND MORRIS

Territorial Behavior

The Norton Reader, p. 510; Shorter Edition, p. 331

"Territorial Behavior" comes from Desmond Morris's *Manwatching: A Field Guide to Human Behavior* (1979). Trained as a zoologist, Morris became keeper of mammals at the London Zoo and a well-known guest on the television talk show circuit. Some find fault with what they claim is his insufficiently critical application of theories about other mammals to humankind; his critics assert, for example, that he emphasizes similarities to such an extent that important differences are neglected. Nonetheless, Morris offers challenging, sometime provocative insights into patterns of human behavior, often establishing undeniable and illuminating parallels.

Analytical Considerations

1. Re: content
   a. What are the three kinds of human territory?
   b. Give an example of a "modern pseudo-tribe."
   c. We all carry with us, everywhere we go, a portable territory called ____________.
   d. What is the difference between a "spectator crowd" and a "rush-hour crowd"?
   e. What is "cocooning"?
2. How does the establishment of territorial rights help avoid social chaos?
3. Why do people display "Territorial Signals"?
4. Have students explain how Morris accounts for the popularity of clubs, gangs, political parties, and fraternities, what he calls "these modern pseudo-tribes."
5. Ask students to what extent they accept Morris's application of patterns of animal behavior to human behavior. Are there dangers involved in this kind of study?
6. Though it may seem obvious, it may be useful to talk about the diagrammatic structure of this essay; "Territorial Behavior" is neatly organized and skillfully developed.

Suggested Writing Assignments

1. Write an essay in which you apply the principles Morris sets forth here to your dormitory or your English class or the setting of your choice.
2. Write an essay based on Analytical Consideration 5.
3. Write an essay in response to Morris's statement "It is one of the tragedies of modern architecture that there has been a standardization of these vital territorial living units [homes]."
4. Compare/contrast Desmond Morris with Robert Finch as writers concerned with the meaning and relevance of parallels between animal life and human behavior.

JUDITH VIORST

Good as Guilt

The Norton Reader, p. 501; Shorter Edition, p. 339

Judith Viorst's "Good as Guilt," a chapter from her book *Necessary Losses*, combines definition and classification with the use of apt examples. Taking as her thesis the idea that guilt can be good as well as bad, Viorst distinguishes one kind from the other, calling the first "appropriate," the second "inappropriate." In effect, she writes an argument advancing the assertion that "we and our world would be monstrous minus guilt." Her persona, which is both knowledgeable and appealingly human, lends credibility to her argument and fosters confidence in her audience.

Analytical Considerations

1. Re: content
   a. Around what age do we begin to develop a conscience?
   b. What is "indiscriminate guilt"?
   c. Who are Ellie and Marvin?
   d. A powerful need to injure oneself or a persistent need to get or to give oneself punishment may indicate what type of guilt?
   e. What is meant by the term "ego ideal"?
2. Ask students to state Viorst's thesis. How does she develop it?
3. Ask students to explain what it means to describe this essay as classification analysis with illustration.
4. How does Viorst define guilt? How many types of guilt does she discuss? Distinguish each.
5. In at least a dozen instances here Viorst uses one-sentence paragraphs, a feature worth exploring. You might begin by asking students to describe the kinds of paragraphs Viorst uses and where she places them. Then focus on how the one-sentence paragraphs work for variety, contrast, and rhetorical effect.
6. With what kinds of material does Viorst illustrate her essay? What is the effect of the rabbi's story? Of quotations from Freud and Buber? Of Viorst's drawing upon common knowledge or experience?
7. Ask students to describe the tone of this essay. Do they find it preachy?

Suggested Writing Assignments

1. Write an essay analyzing Viorst's purpose and audience for this essay.
2. Retaining the same subject and purpose, recast this essay for a significantly different audience.
3. Write an essay in which you argue against Viorst's thesis.
4. Using evidence from your own experience, write an essay illustrating "good" guilt and "bad" guilt.

Additional questions on this essay will be found in the text (NR 509, SE 347).

LEWIS THOMAS

The Long Habit

The Norton Reader, p. 575; Shorter Edition, p. 348

Lewis Thomas is a physician with impressive credentials (former dean of the Yale Medical School, president of the Memorial Sloan-Kettering Center for Cancer Research) and a practiced writer (columnist for the *New England Journal of Medicine*) with a lyric sensitivity.

This selection from his *NEJM* column, "Notes of a Biology Watcher," is at least as much concerned with philosophical and human emotional issues as with scientific ones.

In an essay that combines information and speculation, Lewis Thomas writes about "the only reality in nature of which we can have absolute certainty," death. Like Elisabeth Kübler-Ross, he believes that this "unmentionable, unthinkable" phenomenon must be mentioned and thought about if we are to accept it as an inevitable process faced by all living creatures. Thomas has no desire to prolong life here with technological gadgetry "until we have discovered some satisfactory things to do with the extra time." For him, "dying is an all-right thing to do" not only because it is natural but because he has a biologically based, rather than theologically based, faith in the continuity of consciousness. Characteristically Thomas writes familiarly, but in a controlled, subtle, and superbly moving fashion.

Analytical Considerations

1. What is the "long habit"? What are the source and significance of Thomas's title?
2. Why does "Death on a grand scale . . . not bother us in the same special way" as personal death?
3. Why does Thomas not want to live here "forever"? Has he hit upon a major paradox in contemporary society?
4. Ask students what they think about the adage from folk wisdom "We are born to die." How does science reinforce that observation? (See paragraph 8, "Death is not. . . .)
5. Is this an argument against the use of extraordinary means to prolong "life"?
6. Compare and contrast the observations on death and dying people in "The Long Habit" with those in Elisabeth Kübler-Ross's "On the Fear of Death" (NR 579, SE 352). Are these philosophies compatible? Explain.

Comparative Considerations

1. After reading the four essays by Lewis Thomas in *The Norton Reader*, work toward an appreciation of him as an essayist. What are his concerns? His usual topics? His stylistic characteristics? His rhetorical strategies? His persona? Turn your reading, discussion, previous writing, and reflection into a substantive essay.
2. How does "The Long Habit" illustrate Thomas's central point in "On Magic in Medicine" (NR 450, SE 370)?

Suggested Writing Assignments

1. Write an essay on how "the only reality in nature of which we can have absolute certainty" is dealt with in American culture.
2. Do some research on the phenomenon of the return from death, the so-called Lazarus Syndrome. Then write an essay that describes, evaluates, and perhaps speculates on the data you have uncovered.
3. Thomas seems to believe permanent life, or even extremely prolonged life, is rather undesirable. Why? Can you offer some suggestions for making the lives of old people in our culture more self-fulfilling?

Additional questions on this essay will be found in the text (NR 578, SE 351).

ELISABETH KÜBLER-ROSS

On the Fear of Death

The Norton Reader, p. 579; Shorter Edition, p. 352

Dr. Elisabeth Kübler-Ross, a Swiss psychologist, has written an eloquent and influential text, *On Death and Dying* (1969). A pioneer in reexamining "modern" attitudes on the subject, she has consistently advocated patient-centered approaches that scrupulously protect patients' rights. Though certainly not opposed to the implementation of advanced medical technology whenever necessary, Kübler-Ross opposes rapid-fire, depersonalized care of emergency and terminal cases, asserting that it reveals "our own defensiveness" and deep fear of death. Despite the sensitivity of the subject matter, the essay can generate substantial discussion and writing. (Two books you may want to examine if you choose to teach this essay: *The Hour of Our Death* [1981] by Philippe Ariès and *The American Way of Death* by Jessica Mitford [1963].)

Analytical Considerations

1. Re: content
   a. Kübler-Ross's essay opens with a selection from a poem by ______________.
   b. Kübler-Ross tells us the intended audience for her essay. Describe it.
   c. What is Kübler-Ross's profession?
   d. What is "psychotic depression"?
   e. What is Kübler-Ross's conclusion?
2. Why does Kübler-Ross spend so much time discussing various historical examples?
3. Extract from this essay Kübler-Ross's guidelines for dealing with children and the subject of death.
4. Show how Kübler-Ross uses the techniques of causal analysis and process analysis in the last quarter of her essay.
5. What is the relationship of Tagore's poem to the essay? How can this serve as an example of how to write an effective introduction?
6. Have students relate, then comment on Kübler-Ross's narrative of the death of a farmer in Switzerland. What is its role in the rhetoric of "On the Fear of Death"?
7. Kübler-Ross explicitly states that she has written this essay for "other professional people, for instance, chaplains and social workers." Is her essay geared to an audience of professionals? Why or why not?

Suggested Writing Assignments

1. Write an essay on your own experience of grieving and trying to come to terms with the death of a loved one.
2. Read Lewis Thomas's "The Long Habit" (NR 575, SE 348), and compare his views with those of Kübler-Ross on death in contemporary American society, the nature of death itself, and the potential for an afterlife of sorts.
3. Write about the role of ritual in the grieving process; draw upon your own experience, if possible.
4. Do you think the fear of death increases or decreases with age? Explain in an essay.

Additional questions on this essay will be found in the text (NR 585, SE 358).

ETHICS

SAMUEL L. CLEMENS

Advice to Youth

The Norton Reader, p. 599; Shorter Edition, p. 361

Samuel L. Clemens, probably nineteenth-century America's best satirist, has taken one of the most stuffy and trite literary forms, the graduation/commencement address, and turned it into a devastating parody. His use of irony, his knowledge of the fine points of rhetoric, and his humorous assaults on the ways and attitudes of elders give "Advice to Youth" lasting appeal. Particularly interesting here is Clemens's development of a persona that enables him to achieve considerable rapport with the members of his audience, then and now.

Analytical Considerations

1. This essay needs to be read aloud; ask a student to prepare a reading; this will offer opportunities to talk about pauses and silence, rhythm, and sound appeal.

2. Consider just the first paragraph. What expectations does the speaker create? What kind of tone and context does he establish?

Next, examine paragraphs 2 and 3. Do they continue in the same fashion as paragraph 1? What clues alert the listener/reader to shifts and predict the rest of the essay?

3. Where do signs of Clemens's use of irony first appear? Where and how does he use irony in the rest of the piece? Does he use irony in the same way that Jonathan Swift does in "A Modest Proposal" (NR 807, SE 489)?

4. One occasional difficulty in teaching this selection is that students sometimes see this essay as entirely destructive. They may need to have pointed out the positive values against which the satirist hurls the negatives. One way of getting toward that goal is to ask students to write a one-paragraph statement of the positive values Clemens wants his audience to acquire.

5. Has this speech become dated, or does it retain its impact now, in the late 1980s?

Suggested Writing Assignments

1. Write an essay comparing Clemens and Swift as ironic stylists.

2. Write an essay analyzing the speeches given at your high school graduation, or write the address that should have been given.

3. Review Maya Angelou's "Graduation" (NR 22, SE 11), and write the graduation speech that should have been delivered for her 8th-grade class.

Additional questions on this essay will be found in the text (NR 602, SE 363).

MICHAEL LEVIN

The Case for Torture

The Norton Reader, p. 619; Shorter Edition, p. 364

Michael Levin's essay, which originally appeared in the "My Turn" column of *Newsweek*, makes a case for the use of torture. Though he is careful to clarify and limit the circumstances for such action, here he introduces a controversial subject, likely to produce volatile discussion. Our recent historical heritage, with the wholesale torture of Jews and others by Nazis and the startling use of torture in several contemporary "democracies," may increase the pain of considering this essay for some students and instructors. Nonetheless, this is an issue we should consider. Certainly the application of Levin's ideas would represent a significant change in the way Western democracies operate.

Analytical Considerations

1. Under what circumstances is torture permissible as far as Levin is concerned?
2. Have students outline the structure of Levin's argument, indicating rhetorical procedures and listing his major assertions.
3. Where and how does Levin use assumptions?
4. Do students accept the validity of reasoning from hypothetical cases?
5. Why does Levin use a number of rhetorical questions in "The Case for Torture"?
6. Does Levin see the decision to use torture in ethical terms?
7. Ask students to think about how this essay may reveal attitudes and ideas that typify a particular culture and time. Could it have been written only in late twentieth-century America?

Suggested Writing Assignments

1. Write an argument against Levin's contentions in "The Case for Torture."
2. Extract a particularly controversial assertion from Levin's essay and argue for or against it.

3. Write an essay describing the persona of the writer in "The Case for Torture." What does it have to do with the way you respond to the essay?

Additional questions on this essay will be found in the text (NR 621, SE 366).

BARBARA GRIZZUTI HARRISON

Abortion

Shorter Edition, p. 367

Although Barbara Grizzuti Harrison's title will lead most readers to expect an argument for or against abortion, what the reader gets is much more interesting (since the pros and cons of abortion are painfully familiar to most readers). Harrison's essay is really about the complexity of any ethical or moral stance and the difficulty of maintaining congruence between belief and action. The issue of abortion may have prompted Harrison toward an understanding of the nature of moral choice, but in the essay it is a rhetorical vehicle that carries the reader to Harrison's insights about ethics and morality applicable to a great many other issues.

Analytical Considerations

1. What does Harrison accomplish, or fail to accomplish, in "Abortion"? Judge the worth of the article as both a statement of idea and a piece of writing.
2. Explain how Harrison uses ethical appeal to create an image of herself as a rational, open, nonjudgmental person. Does her persona encourage receptivity to her ideas? Explain.
3. Point out the ways Barbara Grizzuti Harrison uses testimony and authority to develop her essay. Does her selection of authorities seem biased?
4. Review "Abortion" in light of the questions about argumentative discourse in the *Guide* discussion of "Letter from Birmingham Jail" (p. 120). What elements of good arguing does Harrison employ? Is her essay an argument?
5. How does Harrison's use of personal details affect your response to "Abortion"?
6. What does the concept of "authentic ethical decisions" mean to Harrison? To students?

Suggested Writing Topics

1. Using issues other than abortion and giving specific examples

(from personal experience, if you wish), illustrate in an essay how, as one woman quoted in Harrison's article says that "moral decisions always come out of the perspective of being related."

2. Are moral decisions more difficult to make in contemporary America than in a more highly structured or uniform culture? Write an essay expressing your opinion.

3. After reading Michael Levin's "The Case for Torture" (NR 619, SE 364), decide whether either Levin or Harrison or both are ethical relativists. Write an essay on ethical relativism, discussing its possible dangers and benefits.

4. In her concluding statement, Barbara Grizzuti Harrison asserts that "the function of morality is to make one profoundly uncomfortable. . . ." Do traditional systems of morality (e.g., religions, philosophies) function in the way Harrison suggests they should? Explain, in an essay, drawing on specific examples.

LEWIS THOMAS

On Magic in Medicine

The Norton Reader, p. 450; Shorter Edition, p. 370

A sane, steady voice in this age of wonder drugs, Lewis Thomas here assumes the role of a "skeptic in medicine" in discussing modern society's vulnerable and gullible stance toward diseases and cures. Drawing examples from the history of "folk doctrine about disease," in particular from the "Seven Healthy Life Habits," Thomas points out where wishful thinking and the need for a sense of control blind us to the faulty statistical and incomplete scientific evidence underlying many popular cures and preventions. With a light but sure hand Thomas advises us to wait patiently for science to "come in, as it has in the past, with the solid facts."

Analytical Considerations

1. Re: content
    a. What is the average life expectancy for men and women?
    b. Who placed the advertisement for the "Seven Healthy Life Habits" in the *New York Times*?
    c. Those habits are said to add how many years to one's life?
    d. What is "bifurcated ideological appeal"?
    e. What is Thomas's "message"?

2. Ask students to summarize, in one sentence, the point Thomas seeks to establish. Is there a thesis statement containing that point?

3. Have students analyze the strategy Thomas uses in his opening

paragraphs (1 through 3). This, in turn, may lead to a consideration of how Thomas has organized the whole essay.

4. What does Thomas mean by saying, "Tuberculosis was the paradigm"? What is a paradigm? What is its purpose?

5. What audience did Thomas have in mind when he wrote his essay? What features of the text lead to this conclusion? What would be an appropriate context for publication?

7. Is "On Magic in Medicine" a good title for this essay? What does Thomas mean by "magic"?

Suggested Writing Assignments

1. Write an essay in which you prove or disprove Thomas's assertion "When it comes to serious illness, the public tends, understandably, to be more skeptical about the skeptics, more willing to believe the true believers." Use specific examples.

2. Write an analysis of "On Magic in Medicine" as argument. Is Thomas successful in persuading you to embrace his point of view?

3. Imagine that you are a lobbyist for the Blue Cross organization that placed the "Seven Healthy Life Habits" advertisement in the *New York Times*. Write an advertisement/essay for the op-ed page in response to Thomas's criticism.

Additional questions on this essay will be found in the text (NR 454, SE 373).

STEPHEN JAY GOULD

The Terrifying Normalcy of AIDS

The Norton Reader, p. 643; Shorter Edition, p. 374

Here one of the most distinguished contemporary biologists turns his attention to a crisis of pandemic proportions. In the process he develops an essay that uses current events, historical information, and scientific data to support his contentions. This essay might well be titled "The Message of Orlando," for Gould uses Disney's Epcot Center as a metaphor for one of the most salient characteristics of the American attitude: an unqualified confidence in the ability of technology to solve all problems. Gould is at pains to disabuse his reader of that attitude; he asserts that it obscures our vision of AIDS as a "natural phenomenon," a "mechanism." Gould avoids the pitfalls of moralizing about the issue as he argues for a positive, defined approach to the tragedy. "The Terrifying Normalcy of AIDS" is a model of dispassionate, informed analysis combined with compassionate concern.

Analytical Considerations

1. Re: content
   a. What does "pandemic" mean?
   b. What was John Platt's discovery?
   c. Where did the AIDS virus probably originate?
   d. What is "paleopathology"?
   e. Does Gould believe that there is a moral lesson in the AIDS pandemic?

2. Ask students to summarize Gould's article in one sentence; then ask if they can find a thesis statement that expresses their sense of summary.

3. What does Gould mean by calling AIDS "an ordinary natural phenomenon"?

4. Ask students to explain what Gould means by the following statements:
   a. "What a tragedy that our moral stupidity caused us to lose precious time. . . ."
   b. "If AIDS had first been imported from Africa into a Park Avenue apartment, we would not have dithered as the exponential march began."

5. How and why does Gould use Disney's Epcot Center at Orlando, Florida? To what effect?

6. Have students analyze the content and structure of Gould's last three paragraphs. How do they function in the design of the essay? How do they reinforce both thesis and persona?

Suggested Writing Assignments

1. If you have not read Michael Stone's essay "Should Testing for the AIDS Virus Be Mandatory?" (NR646, SE 377), do so. Write an essay in response to Stone's title question, drawing on what you have learned from Gould's essay.

2. Write an essay on Gould's assertion "The message of Orlando –the inevitability of technological solutions–is wrong, and we need to understand why."

MICHAEL STONE

Should Testing for the AIDS Virus Be Mandatory?

The Norton Reader, p. 646; Shorter Edition, p. 377

This section from Michael Stone's lengthy article "Q. and A. on AIDS" from *New York* magazine is a provocative excerpt that can stand on its own as an essay. It is nearly pure exposition, for Stone takes no side on the question but rather sets forth the position of health officials and epidemiologists, on the one hand, and clinical doctors, on the other. Dispassionate, well researched, and informative, "Should Testing for the AIDS Virus Be Mandatory?" presents the essential lines of thought, if not all the evidence wanted, to prepare an argument on the subject. (Elisabeth Kübler-Ross's book *AIDS: The Ultimate Challenge* [1987] would be a useful supplement.)

Analytical Considerations

1. Re: content
   a. What is the overriding objection of health officials and epidemiologists to mandatory testing?
   b. Why are advocates of civil liberties opposed to mandatory testing?
   c. In what two cases do health officials support mandatory testing?
   d. Which state has taken the most aggressive approach to the problem?

2. Ask students to locate an explicit thesis statement here. If they find none, ask them to create one.

3. What is Stone's purpose? Does the text give substantial indications of his audience? If so, describe his "mock reader."

4. Characterize the views of those in favor of mandatory testing and those opposed to it. Where does Stone stand?

5. Have students discern and label the parts of Stone's essay. Do they think it is carefully, clearly, and logically organized? How do they feel about his conclusion?

6. In "The Growing Danger" (NR 650, SE 381) Thomas Murray defines an "ism" as "making unwarranted judgments about people based on irrelevant criteria." Suggest that students consider whether or not "AIDism" exists. If so, what does it mean for everyone, both now and in the near future?

Suggested Writing Assignments

1. Write an essay in response to the question of whether or not testing for the AIDS virus should be mandatory. For whom? When? Administered by whom?

2. Stone's last sentence may be the most provocative in the essay: "Indeed, if heterosexual, white, middle-class Americans no longer regard AIDS as an imminent threat to them, the growing effort to contain it may falter." Consider writing an essay in response to that comment.

3. Write an essay in response to discussion and reflection about Analytical Consideration 6, above.

THOMAS MURRAY

The Growing Danger

The Norton Reader, p. 650; Shorter Edition, p. 381

Thomas Murray's essay deals with complex ethical issues in a simple, clear, and human way. Limiting his discussion of genetic engineering to one specific procedure, the use of a biosynthetically manufactured growth hormone, hGH, Murray describes its applications, then proceeds to raise serious moral questions about such practices. He argues not only against the use of hGH to overcome a perceived disadvantage but also against society's "making unwarranted judgments about people based on irrelevant criteria." In sum, Murray has written a two-pronged argument, interesting because of his evident knowledge of the subject, effective because of his ability to present that knowledge and argue with authority without preaching.

Analytical Considerations

1. Re: content
   a. What is "gene therapy"?
   b. Who is Dr. Martin Cline?
   c. What are "somatic cells"?
   d. What does biosynthetic hGH do?
   e. How does Murray define an "ism"?
2. Ask students to summarize Murray's argument. Is it convincing? Why/why not? How does Murray use evidence?
3. How does Murray distinguish a disease from a disability from a disadvantage? How important are these definitions in his argument?
4. Tone is important here, as in all argument; it is crucial when the topic is sensitive and fraught with moral considerations. Murray manages to create a tone that is calm, measured, and appealingly human; he does not paint a "worst-case scenario." Ask students to describe his tone and persona and to list the means by which he develops them.
5. Direct students' attention to Murray's use of questions. Where and how does he use them? Are they merely rhetorical? Transitional?
6. Have students examine the opening paragraph as an example of an effective introduction. Why and how does he succeed?
7. What is the wisest course in regard to hGH as far as Murray is concerned?

Suggested Writing Assignments

1. Write an essay in which you argue for or against using biosynthetic hGH for nontherapeutic purposes.
2. Write an essay about heightism in contemporary society. To what extent does height matter today? Does our language reflect a preoccupation with height?
3. Review the excerpt from the statement issued by the general secretaries of three national religious organizations in paragraph 2 of Murray's essay. Then write an essay on the last sentence (" 'Those who would play God will be tempted as never before' ").

Additional questions on this essay will be found in the text (NR 655, SE 388).

WILLARD GAYLIN

What You See Is the Real You

The Norton Reader, p. 664; Shorter Edition, p. 386

This brief essay by Willard Gaylin, the president of the Institute of Society, Ethics, and the Life Sciences, offers simply and directly an opinion to counter the generally assumed position of psychiatry that the inner person is truer or more important than the outer. Gaylin speaks to the reader in a straightforward way, using the first and second persons. His approach seems informal but trenchant. One is left with no doubt about where Gaylin stands; the edge in the persona's voice is consistently maintained through the essay, so that both the controversial nature of the opinion and, as a consequence, the opinion itself command the reader's attention. In the world in which other people have to live and in the world of morality the way one behaves is what counts. Thus, the person one is–the "real" person, in Gaylin's deliberately simplified terminology–is the person who is seen.

Analytical Considerations

1. Re: content
   a. What is Gaylin's profession?
   b. What is the difference between the inner person and the outer person as far as Gaylin is concerned?
   c. Gaylin establishes an analogy between psychoanalysis and Xray technology for what purpose?
   d. Gaylin speculates on the "similarity of the unconscious constellations" between what two men?
   e. Who is Father Flanagan?

2. Gaylin's conclusion in "What You See Is the Real You" suggests that the psychological view of human behavior has no social value. Argue against this position by discussing ways in which psychology has contributed, or may contribute, to our society.

3. Do students agree with Gaylin's estimate (paragraph 8) that "You are for the most part what you seem to be, not what you would wish to be, nor, indeed, what you believe yourself to be"?

4. Examine the range and effect of references used by Gaylin. Do they constitute substantial, convincing evidence? What do they say about the author?

5. Is Gaylin's use of repetition an effective rhetorical device?

Suggested Writing Assignments

1. Turn your response to Analytical Consideration 3 into an essay.

2. Write an essay in response to Kurt Vonnegut's definition of the human person (paragraph 5). Formulate a definition of your own in the process.

3. Write an argument against Gaylin's contention in "What You See Is the Real You."

Additional questions on this essay will be found in the text (NR 666, SE 388).

HISTORY

WALT WHITMAN

Death of Abraham Lincoln

The Norton Reader, p. 696; Shorter Edition, p. 389

Arguably the finest poet of nineteenth-century America, Walt Whitman was also a journalist and essayist of some accomplishment. A man of strong democratic political convictions, he championed the cause of what he called genuineness, and he believed in the common man; during the Civil War he served as a wound dresser and came to know the horrors of violence firsthand. Abraham Lincoln became a powerful emblematic figure for Whitman, who wrote a number of pieces about the sixteenth president, including an elegy, "When Lilacs Last in the Dooryard Bloom'd," and this essay, "Death of Abraham Lincoln."

Analytical Considerations

1. Re: content
   a. What was so unusual about the way the crowds in New York City received Lincoln?
   b. At what hotel did Lincoln stay?
   c. What source did Whitman use for writing his account of Lincoln's death?
   d. What was the title of the play Lincoln saw on the evening of April 14, 1865?
   e. How will the death of Lincoln serve leading historians and dramatists of the future as far as Whitman is concerned?

2. Ask students to state in one sentence what Whitman attempts to do with Lincoln in this essay.

3. Does the physical description Whitman offers of Lincoln in paragraph 2 create a vivid picture of the president-elect? How?

4. Have students notice the way Whitman constructs his sentences, particularly where he places subjects, verbs, and adjectives. What does he attempt to do in dramatic and poetic terms? Does he succeed? Sentence length needs to be studied as well; do sentences as long as the one beginning "Through the general hum following" (paragraph 11) and "When centuries hence" (paragraph 19) function effectively?

5. How does Whitman use negation and parallelism as rhetorical strategies in "Death of Abraham Lincoln"?

6. Have students read "When Lilacs Last in the Dooryard Bloom'd" for class discussion, comparing/contrasting it with this

essay. Suggest that they think not only about subject, purpose, and audience but also about imagery, rhythm, and diction.

Suggested Writing Assignments

1. Write an essay in response to Analytical Consideration 6 above.
2. Write an essay about "Death of Abraham Lincoln" as an exercise in creating an American mythology. What is the value of such a mythology? Do we need it? Where? How?
3. Write an essay in which you test the accuracy of Whitman's view of Lincoln and his prediction about how "leading historians and dramatists" would use him. Has he become an emblematic figure to represent the "absolute extirpation and erasure of slavery from the States"?

Additional questions on this essay will be found in the text (NR 703, SE 396).

HANNAH ARENDT

Denmark and the Jews

The Norton Reader, p. 714; Shorter Edition, p. 397

Perhaps the most important theme of Hannah Arendt's *Eichmann in Jerusalem: A Report on the Banality of Evil* (1963), from which this selection comes, is that of the "ordinariness of evil." Adolf Eichmann regarded his role in the infamous Nazi "final solution to the Jewish question" as that of a "functionary." At his trial in Jerusalem, Arendt suggests, he most regretted having been ill used by superiors. According to Arendt, his inability to accept much personal blame was not extraordinary or abnormal, for evil apparently loses its character as evil when it is assimilated into the normal routine of living and working. It is against this background that Arendt sets the Danish reaction to the Nazi program of destruction.

Arendt contends in this selection that the Danes provided the "only case we know of in which the Nazis met with *open* native resistance." This point (and several others in her book) have been criticized by other observers. What Arendt does to marshal support for her views is fill her discussion to repletion with facts and statistics which lend an air of authority to *all* that she says. Too, she studiously avoids emotionalism in presenting her views. Whether or not one wholly accepts Arendt's extreme and rigid contentions, her general views (about the Danes, about the "ordinariness" of evil) provide fascinating vantage points for discussion.

Analytical Considerations

1. "Denmark and the Jews" is partially narrative in organization. Does the narrative have a climax? Where does it occur? What is the effect of being told the implications of the story before learning the story?
2. The tendency to think the Danes moral heroes seems an inevitable effect of this essay. Is there evidence that Arendt tries to temper this opinion, to make us see the Danes as something other or as less than heroes (this does not imply seeing them as villains)?
3. Read the essay carefully for evidence of Arendt's bitterness about the history and fate of European Jews. What are her chief means of controlling this bitterness so that its appearance is effective?
4. Distinguish the facts in Arendt's essay from the views of the author. Then decide how well the facts support the views. In all cases can you clearly say that Arendt's ideas have been drawn by valid induction?
5. Evaluate the final paragraph of "Denmark and the Jews." Which statements in the paragraph are matters of record? Which are matters of contention? How well are the matters of contention prepared for by preceding sections? Explain in detail.
6. Why does Arendt describe the Danes as a nation or as a group instead of focusing on individuals? In view of her purpose, is there a rhetorical advantage in so viewing them?
7. Does Arendt regard her subject as primarily a moral or an ethical one? If so, what facets of the discussion suggest this view? How valid as history is Arendt's moral approach to her subject?

Suggested Writing Topics

1. If Nazis like Eichmann exhibit the "ordinariness of evil," then the Danes exhibit the "ordinariness of good." Drawing from your own experience, write an essay in which you support, refute, or evaluate this assertion.
2. Compare Arendt's ideas on "resistance based on principle" and "nonviolent action" with Martin Luther King's in "Letter from Birmingham Jail" (NR 792, SE 473).
3. Using "Denmark and the Jews" as a basis, construct a code of conduct for nonviolent resistance to any unjust authority or unjust policy.
4. Write a historical narrative of some person or group who in some vital or violent controversy held to principle and proved to be exceptional.

MICHAEL ARLEN

Griefspeak

The Norton Reader, p. 719; Shorter Edition, p. 402

Michael Arlen writes regularly about television, most often for the *New Yorker.* He and John O'Connor of the *New York Times* are probably our most respected critics of the medium. "Griefspeak" is not an easy essay, for Arlen loads the piece with masses of details–facts, comments, references–that may present initial obstacles. A second reading helps clarify both content and techniques considerably. Arlen has used television coverage of a specific three-day event, the assassination and funeral of Robert F. Kennedy, as a basis for social commentary. In describing the indecency, poverty of thought, and dependence on clichés and disconnected trivia that characterized TV coverage in June 1968, Arlen has exposed the radical insufficiency of the "complete" instant information this medium claims to offer. Indeed, his style mimics television: a barrage of scenes and meaningless commentary hurled at the reader who finally asks, "What do I know?"

Analytical Considerations

1. What is "griefspeak"?
2. Have students give a one-sentence summary of Arlen's criticism of television.
3. Ask students to describe the kinds of information Arlen supplies. From what vantage point does he write?
4. What is Arlen's thesis? Why has he placed it where he has?
5. Why has Arlen written the whole essay in one paragraph?
6. Why did television commentators discuss the "irony of the situation"?
7. Why is this selection included in the "History" section of *The Norton Reader*?
8. Ask students to determine Arlen's purpose in writing "Griefspeak." Suggest that they consider the possibility that this essay is an implicit argument.

Suggested Writing Assignments

1. Write an essay in which you argue for or against the proposition that television coverage of news has enhanced people's understanding of "history in the making."
2. Watch the evening news on one or two major networks for a week. Record the events covered, the sequence of stories, and a sense of the spoken report accompanying items (characteristic words, phrases). Write an essay about the way news is covered,

comparing and contrasting the two networks you have followed, or write an essay about the vision of life in the United States offered by television journalists. Be sure to include some discussion of the ways in which newswriters and commentators view their audience.

Additional questions on this essay will be found in the text (NR 721, SE 404).

MICHAEL HERR

"How Bad Do You Want to Get to Danang?"

The Norton Reader, p. 722; Shorter Edition, p. 405

" 'How Bad Do You Want to Get to Danang?' " comes from Michael Herr's documentary about the Vietnam War, *Dispatches* (1977). The selection is raw in places but evocative throughout. Its value lies more in its narrative and descriptive power than in its quality as an essay in any conventional sense. In its shifting focus and rapid-fire rendering of a slice of life and death, " 'How Bad Do You Want to Get to Danang?' " achieves a cinematic quality, its style becoming a metaphor for the experience of war.

Analytical Considerations

1. Herr's essay is graphic and powerful; you might begin by soliciting students' responses to the piece. What does the essay reveal about the human face of war? Does this excerpt from *Dispatches* make students want to read the whole book? Why?
2. The title *Dispatches* has meaning on both textual and contextual levels. Discuss.
3. Ask students to describe the narrator. Is he a soldier? An officer? A journalist? What is the effect of Herr's use of the first-person voice in his essay?
4. Herr's eye, like the lens of the camera, rapidly takes in the sights and sounds of the war in horrible detail. How does Herr use languages to create vivid images? What is the role of description, snatches of conversation, graphic language, military terms?

Suggested Writing Assignments

1. Written in 1977, *Dispatches* continues to be widely read—an indication of how strongly the American experience in Vietnam resonates in our culture and memory. Other books like David Morrell's *First Blood* (1982) and Loren Baritz's *Backfire* (1985) and films like *Platoon* and *Apocalypse Now* remind us of this chapter in

recent history. Write an essay in which you attempt to account for America's tenacious interest in works on Vietnam.

2. Read and review *Dispatches* for the audience of your choice.

3. Choose an event in history or in your own life from which to create a narrative that will give your readers a sense of immediacy. Use description, conversation, personal reflection to give your writing power.

KILDARE DOBBS

The Shatterer of Worlds

The Norton Reader, p. 725; Shorter Edition, p. 408

"The Shatterer of Worlds" is a clear, direct journalistic essay relating the story of a fifteen-year-old Japanese girl who was in Hiroshima on the fateful day when an American B-29 dropped the first atomic bomb on a civilian population. With crisp detachment, Kildare Dobbs records the impact of this catastrophic event on the life of one Japanese family, caught, like other families, in the midst of near-apocalyptic destruction. Dobbs's narrative pattern alternates between young Emiko's story and that of the crew of the *Enola Gay*. This technique does more than provide two different perspectives on the same event: It juxtaposes the dispassionate and amoral stance of the flight crew ("We turned the ship so that we could observe the results"; "There'll be a short intermission while we bomb our target") with the emotional and physical devastation of the residents of Hiroshima. The moral resonance of this juxtaposition is keen. Throughout, Dobbs's narrative is enhanced by his careful attention to detail.

Analytical Considerations

1. Re: content
   a. Who was Emiko?
   b. Name the U.S. B-29 that carried the world's first operational atomic bomb.
   c. Why were Emiko and her sister going to Hiroshima?
   d. Who did the final assembly of the bomb?
   e. On August 11 what other Japanese city suffered the same fate as Hiroshima?

2. Ask students to describe in detail the impact of the atomic bomb on Emiko and her family.

3. Ask students to locate Dobbs's thesis. What has he expressed it in three sentences?

4. Ask students what the word "obscene" means to them. Then ask if it has the same meaning in paragraph 3 of this essay. This is a

particularly interesting word to trace in the *Oxford English Dictionary*; you might assign the task to students or prepare a handout of your own.

5. Trace the development of Dobbs's narrative?
6. How would students describe the tone of this essay? Why has Dobbs avoided making judgments?
7. What is Dobbs's purpose in writing "The Shatterer of Worlds"? Ask students what they would consider the appropriate context for its publication.

Suggested Writing Assignments

1. Write an essay comparing/contrasting this essay with Jonathan Schell's "The Destructive Power of a One-Megaton Bomb on New York City" (NR 472, SE 310).
2. What role do graphs and statistics have in rendering an account of cataclysmic events such as the bombing of Hiroshima? What role do personal narratives of such events have in our perception of them? Respond, in an essay, to diverse accounts of a recent or historic event.

JOAN DIDION

On Keeping a Notebook

The Norton Reader, p. 731; Shorter Edition, p. 414

From an entry in her own notebook Joan Didion writes about the process of reconstructing not only the event recorded but also a sense of herself at the time of the event. This essay provides an unusual opportunity to observe the literary artist at work, exploring one aspect of her art and a significant dimension of herself, for writing enables Didion to discover who she is. Reviewing entries in her notebook allows her to "keep on nodding terms with the people [she] used to be." Her essay, a reflective commentary on the significance of a ritual she has practiced since the age of five, is honest, uncompromising, and challenging.

Analytical Considerations

1. Re: content
   a. Who was the woman in the plaid silk dress from Peck & Peck?
   b. Didion's first notebook was a "Big Five" given to her by ______________.
   c. What is the significance of a fictitious cracked crab here?
   d. When did she write "On Keeping a Notebook"?

2. Why does Joan Didion keep a notebook? What do the "bits of the mind's string too short to use" do for her?

3. Ask students to summarize the process Didion describes here.

4. At what point does the reader realize that the woman in the plaid dress is Didion herself?

5. How does Didion use questions in paragraph 4?

6. Do students agree with Didion when she says, "I think we are well advised to keep on nodding terms with the people we used to be whether we find them attractive company or not."

7. Why does the distinction between what happened and what might have happened not matter for Didion? What does it tell us about the reconstructive powers of memory?

Comparative Considerations

In an essay titled "Why I Write," Joan Didion has noted: "I write entirely to find out what I'm thinking, what I'm looking at, what I see and what it means." In the same essay she reveals that "certain images shimmer" for her and that this picture determines the "arrangement of words." Apply these comments to "On Keeping a Notebook" as well as to "On Going Home" (NR 69, SE 40), "Salvador" (NR 464, SE 302), and "Georgia O'Keeffe" (NR 1098, SE 673). With some guided discussion, students should be able to develop a sense of Didion's literary esthetic and practice. You might assign an essay on "Joan Didion: One Writer's Sense of Style and Purpose."

Suggested Writing Assignments

1. Keep a notebook for a week or so; carry it with you and record what you like. At the end of the week review it. Then write an analysis and commentary on your notebook. Do you share anything with Didion?

2. Write an essay in response to Didion's observation that "we are well advised to keep on nodding terms with the people we used to be whether we find them attractive company or not."

Additional questions on this essay will be found in the text (NR 737, SE 419).

VIRGINIA WOOLF

The New Biography

The Norton Reader, p. 738; Shorter Edition, p. 420

"The New Biography" is at once a historical account of the art of biography, a book review of Harold Nicolson's *Some People*, and an argument for a new form of biography that combines the substance of fact with the techniques of fiction. Virginia Woolf's capsule history of lesser and greater biographers from Mrs. Hutchinson to James Boswell to Lytton Strachey to Harold Nicolson is a statement of personal taste that evolves into a personal response to the twentieth-century reader's desire for writing that melds "into one seamless whole" the writer's sensibility and style, the "granite-like" truths of the subject's life, and the "rainbow-like" qualities that give the life, and the writing, their force.

Analytical Considerations

1. Re: content
   a. Who was Sir Sidney Lee?
   b. In the "old days," biography consisted of a series of ______________.
   c. Who made significant changes in the art of writing biography in the late eighteenth century?
   d. What was the contribution of "Mr. Strachey" to the art?
   e. What book does Woolf choose to illustrate the "new biography"?
2. What is the "new biography"?
3. What is the "truth which biography demands"?
4. Ask students if it is possible to write a biography that is the "truthful transmission of personality."
5. Do people still read biography? Why? What kinds?
6. Have students extract a short list of the principles for writing biography from "The New Biography."
7. How does Sir Sidney Lee serve Woolf in this essay?
8. Let students plot, in summary fashion, the changes in writing biography from Izaak Walton to James Boswell to Lytton Strachey to Harold Nicolson.
9. Have some of the ideas Woolf here expresses been carried too far by modern biographers? For example, do biographers get too close to their subjects, or do they use the techniques of fiction to such an extent that the result is not a "truthful transmission"?
10. Does Woolf balance her estimate of the advantages of the "Nicolson method" with some consideration of its disadvantages?
11. Let students describe the following: Woolf's subject; her audience; her persona in "The New Biography."

Comparative Considerations

1. Analyze and evaluate, according to the principles of "The New Biography," Virginia Woolf's "My Father: Leslie Stephen" (NR 146, SE 83).

2. "In Search of a Room of One's Own" (NR 1053, SE 650) offers the opportunity to see Woolf at work on a double biography, of the historical William Shakespeare, on the one hand, and the fictional Judith Shakespeare, on the other. Examine both portraits as examples of the "new biography."

Suggested Writing Assignments

1. Investigate two biographies of Virginia Woolf; in the interest of time you might use two standard reference works such as *An Encyclopedia of British Women Writers* and the *Dictionary of Literary Biography.* Write an essay comparing/contrasting the two; try to discern the principles of selection and evaluation that guided each writer; evaluate both, and determine which is better and why.

2. Read one of the studies in Lytton Strachey's *Eminent Victorians.* Then write an analysis of the art of biography as practiced by Strachey; give proper attention to considerations like subject, purpose, audience, persona, and development.

3. Choose someone you know well as your subject. Interview that person with the aim of writing a brief "new biography," keeping in mind Woolf's guidelines for truthful and lively biography.

Additional questions on this essay will be found in the text (NR 743, SE 425).

FRANCES FITZGERALD

Rewriting American History

The Norton Reader, p. 744; Shorter Edition, p. 426

Frances FitzGerald is a talented journalist, popularly known for her account of the Vietnam War *Fire in the Lake*. The essay "Rewriting American History" is actually one of three parts of a long essay that appeared serially in the *New Yorker* in the winter of 1979 and was later included in her book *America Revised.* This segment is, for the most part, a highly detailed comparison and contrast between history textbooks of the 1950s and contemporary history texts. Interesting in their own right, the comparison and contrast lead nevertheless to what may interest the reader even more: general commentary on the nature of history as a discipline, which accounts for the changes in texts and history, and personal remarks about the mind's yearning for permanence and order.

Analytical Considerations

1. Re: content
   a. To what generation does Frances Fitzgerald belong?
   b. Who is George McJunkin?
   c. Who is Henry B. Gonzalez?
   d. Why did history textbooks change?
   e. Cite one way in which the physical appearance of history textbooks has changed.

2. Ask students to summarize FitzGerald's essay in one paragraph; then ask several students to read their paragraphs aloud. See what kind of discussion develops.

3. Frances FitzGerald relies mainly on the mode of comparison and contrast to show how American history has been "rewritten." By focusing on two paragraphs, perhaps the one beginning "Poor Columbus!" and the one beginning "The political diversity," demonstrate how the comparison and contrast work.

4. Analyze any one section of "Rewriting American History" to show how FitzGerald defines by example. Possibilities include the section on the political diversity of textbooks today and the section on the physical appearance of textbooks today.

5. Explain how FitzGerald's essay uses the strategy of defining by analysis, as well as defining by example and defining by comparison and contrast. Is it common for these strategies to work together so that it is rather difficult to isolate one from another?

6. What is FitzGerald's understanding of "history"?

7. Ask students to label, according to function, each paragraph in "Rewriting American History."

8. Why do human beings need to create "history"?

9. Evaluate the design and impact of FitzGerald's conclusion.

10. Ask students if FitzGerald's essay implies that we will never be able to (re)construct history, that we will be able to produce only histories that have no lasting place or value.

Suggested Writing Assignments

1. What is history?

2. Write an essay based on comparing and contrasting the same episode from American history as presented in three textbooks, each written during a different decade; be certain to select texts written for the same grade level.

3. To what extent do history textbooks, or any other history books, present "truths"?

4. It appears that the process of rewriting American history may

have taken a good deal of the romance and myth from the subject. Is that good or bad or both?

Additional questions on this essay will be found in the text (NR 750, SE 432).

EDWARD HALLETT CARR

The Historian and His Facts

The Norton Reader, p. 751; Shorter Edition, p. 433

Edward Hallett Carr's "The Historian and His Facts" is a classic essay in the field of historiography. Chapter 13 of Charles Kay Smith's *Styles and Structures* (1974) has informed my teaching of this essay for years, and so, with his kind permission, I offer a condensed version of it. My summary does not do justice to the fullness of Smith's thought; I encourage you to read the chapter yourself.

Carr's essay illustrates the classical rhetoric of synthesis: First, he presents the nineteenth-century assumption that history is a series of self-evident inductions based on all available facts (thesis); then he offers the twentieth-century assumption that history has no objective facts but consists rather of interpretation; and finally, rejecting both, he creates a synthesis of the two by asserting that history is a tension or process of interaction between fact and interpretation. Smith calls Carr's method of organizing his writing "assumptive style," and that is the clearest way of getting to the heart of "The Historian and His Facts."

Analytical Considerations

1. Re: content
   a. Textual clues indicate that "The Historian and His Facts" was originally a ______________ given at ______________.
   b. Who was Gustav Stresemann?
   c. Who invented the term "philosophy of history"?
   d. What was A. L. Rowse's complaint about Sir Winston Churchill's book on World War I *The World Crisis*?
   e. How does Carr define "history" in this essay?
2. Have students state Carr's subject, purpose, and audience in one sentence.
3. What does the narrative of Stresemann's papers illustrate?
4. How does Carr define "history"?
5. How does Carr develop and support thesis, antithesis, and synthesis in "The Historian and His Facts"?
6. Carr does not write what students might consider standard history (nor, for that matter, do the great historians like Thucydides,

Fernand Braudel, and Michel Foucault). One distinguishing feature of Carr's essay is his use of metaphor. Ask students where and how he uses metaphor (e.g., the fish market metaphor, theological metaphor, biblical metaphor). What is the effect of metaphorical language in an essay on historiography?

Suggested Writing Assignments

1. Write an essay about how Frances FitzGerald's "Rewriting American History" (NR 744, SE 426) could be read as a response to Carr, or write an essay comparing/contrasting FitzGerald's and Carr's senses of "history."
2. Write an essay of definition for an important and disputed term, following the thesis-antithesis-synthesis pattern used by Carr in "The Historian and His Facts."
3. Respond to the question "What is history?" in an essay of your own.

Additional questions on this essay will be found in the text (NR 766, SE 449).

POLITICS AND GOVERNMENT

GEORGE ORWELL

Shooting an Elephant

The Norton Reader, p. 768; Shorter Edition, p. 450

George Orwell's essay, really a narrative about role playing, has become a classic for its extraordinary description and for its clear articulation of a particular moral dilemma. It might be helpful to acquaint students both with the context of anticolonialism in Britain's Asian colonies and with some biographical details concerning Orwell, before and immediately after his time in the imperial police force in Burma during the 1920s. "Shooting an Elephant" is a crucial chapter in Orwell's intellectual autobiography and should be seen in that context as well as others.

Analytical Considerations

1. Re: content
   a. Where does this narrative take place?
   b. What does Orwell mean by the "dirty work of Empire"?
   c. Why was it a serious matter to shoot an elephant?
   d. How many shots did it take to kill the elephant?
   e. Why did Orwell shoot the elephant?

2. You might begin class discussion with question e, above. The responses should help probe to the central issues of the essay here. You might lead discussion to the cultural and ethical aspects of this essay by asking students to focus on two excerpts: (1) "The owner was furious, but he was only an Indian and could do nothing"; (2) ". . . an elephant was worth more than any damn Coringhee coolie."

3. Ask students why this essay might well have been placed in the "Ethics" section of the *Reader.*

4. Have students analyze "Shooting an Elephant" according to the principles Orwell himself sets down in "Politics and the English Language" (NR 353, SE 241).

5. To what effect does Orwell use irony in the first paragraph?

6. Consider paying some attention to how Orwell uses the device of delayed action in paragraphs 5 through 10. Why? Is it just to have rhetoric mirror thought and experience? Does he use the strategy of purposeful delay elsewhere?

Suggested Writing Assignments

1. Rewrite this narrative from the viewpoint of one of the Burmese natives. (Note to instructors: You might choose to assign this to all students before discussing "Shooting an Elephant" in class; it often proves to be a good means of getting at the heart of the text.)
2. Write an essay about a particular experience that brought you insight about yourself and/or others. Has there been a time when unavoidable role playing taught you something?
3. Read Ngũgĩ wa Thiong'o's "Decolonizing the Mind" (NR 775, SE 457), and write an essay about what it might mean in relation to "Shooting an Elephant."
4. What do you believe is the purpose or effect of Orwell's essay? Is it personal catharsis? Political analysis and warning? Morality lesson or parable? (Is it all these things?) Express your ideas in an essay.

Additional questions on this essay will be found in the text (NR 774, SE 456).

NGŨGĨ WA THIONG'O

Decolonizing the Mind

The Norton Reader, p. 775; Shorter Edition, p. 457

This is a complex and important essay written in prose that is occasionally difficult. It might best be approached by providing a map or outline for reading beforehand, indicating the three-part division of the essay and emphasizing that the middle section of sociolinguistic analysis from a Marxist point of view is integral to understanding the writer's argument. In his exploration of the relationship between language and culture, Ngũgĩ wa Thiong'o discusses elements of linguistics that may require explanation. Likewise, the political values may need clarification. Nonetheless, "Decolonizing the Mind" repays the effort necessary to get at its argument. Furthermore, its use of African context begins to fill in some of the gaps in students' perceptions of the world. This essay should stimulate further discussion of the ways in which language and culture are tied together.

Analytical Considerations

1. Re: content
   a. What is the author's native language?

b. Why did stories about the hare appeal to the author and his friends?
c. What was the key examination for moving from primary school to secondary school and from secondary school to university?
d. What does "Catching them young" mean in the context of this essay?
e. Who is Léopold Sédar Senghor?

2. What does Ngũgĩ wa Thiong'o mean by the "dual character of language"?

3. Ask students to determine what Ngũgĩ wa Thiong'o considers the root cause of many problems in Africa.

4. Ask students to explain the following remarks taken from "Decolonizing the Mind":

a. "Language as culture is the collective memory bank of a people's experience in history."
b. "The domination of a people's language by the languages of the colonizing nations was crucial to the domination of the mental universe of the colonized."
c. "It is the final triumph of a system of domination when the dominated start singing its virtues."

5. Why is Ngũgĩ wa Thiong'o so scornful of Léopold Senghor and Chinua Achebe? Is his scorn justified? In what terms?

6. Ngũgĩ wa Thiong'o and Dr. Hastings Banda represent polar approaches to a problem. Consider the merits of each approach. Does one have greater merit than the other?

7. Ask students to divide the essay into large functional sections and to talk about how these sections serve the overall design of the essay.

8. Ask who the writer of "Decolonizing the Mind" is insofar as you can determine it strictly from the text.

Suggested Writing Assignments

1. Write an essay in which you design and explain the system of education that would have been most beneficial to Ngũgĩ wa Thiong'o in 1952.

2. Write an essay in which you describe what you have learned from "Decolonizing the Mind." Has Ngũgĩ wa Thiong'o caused you to think about topics you have not previously considered, to think again about topics you have considered?

3. Do some research on Dr. Hastings Banda or Chinua Achebe or Léopold Senghor. Then write a response to Ngũgĩ wa Thiong'o from the perspective of one of these three men.

4. Women are significantly absent from Ngũgĩ wa Thiong'o's text. Write an essay in which you characterize their lot under the system described in "Decolonizing the Mind"; you might use Virginia

Woolf's strategy of creating a fictional sister (see her "In Search of a Room of One's Own" [NR 1053, SE 650]) as a device of your own.

Additional questions on this essay will be found in the text (NR 787, SE 466).

CHARLES R. MORRIS

Civil Disobedience

The Norton Reader, p. 785; Shorter Edition, p. 467

From Chapter 3, "Politics at the Edge of Morality," in his book *A Time of Passion: America, 1960-1980,* Charles R. Morris's essay offers a critical assessment of the theoretical stances used to defend the practice of civil disobedience. Morris's tone is dispassionate, at times mildly mocking, as he analyzes the thinking of advocates of civil disobedience–Martin Luther King, Jr., Mahatma Gandhi, John Rawls, Henry David Thoreau, and the individuals who came to prominence in the 1960s, Howard Zinn and H. Rap Brown–pointing up inconsistency, shortsightedness, and unrealistic assumptions that waken arguments for "legitimate" civil disobedience.

Analytical Considerations

1. Re: content
   a. How did Henry David Thoreau protest American involvement in the war with Mexico in 1848?
   b. During what time in history did civil disobedience become "something of an intellectual industry"?
   c. Martin Luther King, Jr.'s understanding of "legitimate" civil disobedience came from the writings of ____________.
   d. What was the "logic of Nuremberg"?
   e. What is "pragmatism"?

2. Does Morris believe that civil disobedience is ever permissible? Under what circumstances? Is civil disobedience a legitimate tactic to advance the cause of civil rights?

3. Morris is a strong presence in this essay, but only once does he refer to himself directly ("Some of the attempts were ingenious; in my view, none of them was wholly successful"). Identify passages where Morris's judgment is implicit. How does he communicate his opinion? What is his stance toward civil disobedience? Do you think Morris is an idealist? An activist? An observer?

4. What problem does Morris perceive when individual conscience is the sole arbiter of behavior in the face of perceived injustice? Do students agree?

5. Ask students to detail the strategy of Morris's opening

paragraph. Is it a procedure he uses again? Where and to what effect?

6. For what purpose(s) does Morris use examples in the first part of his essay?

7. Ask students to evaluate "Civil Disobedience" as an essay. Have them identify Morris's statement, means of development, persona. Is it a successful essay and convincing argument? Why or why not?

Suggested Writing Assignments

1. Morris sets the stage for his essay with mention of America's tradition of placing moral concerns over political ones. King's "Letter from Birmingham Jail" (NR 792, SE 473) supports this assertion. Do you agree with Morris that America is a nation devoted to the "moral"? Using examples from recent history, defend your point of view in an essay.

2. Read selections from Thoreau's writings on civil disobedience, and test the validity of Morris's assertion that "Thoreau was more quirky than principled, and admitted that he enjoyed picking and choosing which laws to obey."

3. The essential tension in Morris's essay and in the issue of civil disobedience generally lies between the individual conscience and the laws formulated for the common good. When, if ever, do you believe that civil disobedience is permissible? Is violence a legitimate tactic to bring about change?

Additional questions on this essay will be found in the text (NR 788, SE 469).

RALPH W. CONANT

The Justification of Civil Protest, Nonviolent and Violent

The Norton Reader, p. 788; Shorter Edition, p. 470

An excerpt from an article published in the *American Scholar* in 1968, "The Justification of Civil Protest, Nonviolent and Violent" offers both a clear and straightforward exercise in definition and an example of argument by assumption which students should read closely for its strategy and validity. Ralph W. Conant first enumerates the circumstances under which civil disobedience is justified, indeed is required by the strict standards of citizenship. He supports his definitions of civil disobedience and of citizenship with testimony from outside authorities. Conant's tone is matter-of-fact, as if no thinking reader would see cause to disagree with his assertions. In the second part of his essay, on violent civil protest,

Conant strikes a more persuasive tone, presenting the widely-held values of peace, patriotism, and freedom as worthy of protection through nonviolent protest and, when other means are exhausted, through violence. He concludes, in a moderate and almost legalistic tone, with a reassertion of government's right to protect property and punish insurrection. The reader is left with the sense that Conant's views, including his justification of violence, strike a thoughtful, historically informed balance between individual conscience and the common good as determined by law and upheld by government.

Analytical Considerations

1. Ask students to analyze Conant's argument in favor of civil protest involving violence. Is he authoritative? Is he persuasive? On what evidence does he base his justification of violent action? How does he make his stance on violence seem reasoned and moderate?
2. Does Conant consider nonviolent civil disobedience an effective instrument for social change? Do students agree with him?
3. Have students describe Conant's sense of what citizenship in a democracy involves.
4. Encourage students to study paragraph 1 and describe what they have learned from its word choice, syntax, and tone. What kinds of expectations does Conant create? For whom is he writing? Does his tone shift within the piece?
5. Compare Conant's means of supporting his position on nonviolent protest (definition, references to academic and political authority) with his means of supporting his position on violent civil protest. Do students see a shift in strategy? Why?
6. You may wish to explore the moral dimensions of Conant's remarks. Could this selection have been put in the "Ethics" section of *The Norton Reader*? What makes "The Justification of Civil Protest, Nonviolent and Violent" a moral statement?

Suggested Writing Assignments

1. Write an essay in which you apply Conant's criteria for nonviolent civil disobedience to Martin Luther King, Jr.'s defense of the actions of civil rights activists in "Letter from Birmingham Jail" (NR 792, SE 473).
2. Conant's remarks are part of a larger cultural document produced by events in the United States during the 1960s. Do some research on those events; get a sense of the times; then write an essay in which you demonstrate just how "The Justification of Civil Protest" is a cultural document spawned by the historical context.
3. Write an essay in support of Conant's position that civil protest can justifiably involve violence by applying his argument to a situation in the news today.

4. Write a critical analysis of Conant's position on nonviolent and violent civil protest. Charles R. Morris's "Civil Disobedience" (NR 785, SE 467) will offer a point of departure for your thinking. Is Conant's position well reasoned? Can it stand the test of time? Does it support both individual rights and the shared goal of stable, effective government?

Additional questions on this essay will be found in the text (NR 791, SE 473).

MARTIN LUTHER KING, JR.

Letter from Birmingham Jail

The Norton Reader, p. 792; Shorter Edition, p. 473

Without doubt the most important figure in the American civil rights movement, Martin Luther King, Jr., has achieved even greater stature since his death. "Letter from Birmingham Jail" was written in response to a published statement by eight Birmingham, Alabama, clergymen who supported the goals of the civil rights movement but criticized King for his "unwise and untimely" direct-action campaigns. King's letter is a cogent, argumentative defense of his position, an essay which rises to full and dramatic force without ever becoming strident, sarcastic, or uncontrolled. King explains his own ideas and defends the black cause before extending the embrace of his letter in a plea for universal brotherhood and a life in accord with the message of the Gospels. "Letter from Birmingham Jail" is more than a powerful cultural document. In its depth, development, diction, precision, and tone, it is a rhetorical model of significant accomplishment.

Analytical Considerations

1. Re: content
    a. Why did Martin Luther King write this letter? For whom?
    b. To what New Testament figure does King liken himself?
    c. Who was Eugene ("Bull") Connor?
    d. What was the 1954 decision of the Supreme Court about?
    e. Why was King disappointed with white moderates?
2. Consider King's "Letter" as argument. Students' understanding of argumentative essays and facility for writing them might be developed through comparison of King's strategies with those found in such essays as Jonathan Swift's "A Modest Proposal" (NR 807, SE 489) and Niccolò Machiavelli's "The Morals of the Prince" (NR 815, SE 497).

You might use the questions below as bases for discussing the similarities and differences in argumentative techniques among essays:

a. Is the argument logically and convincingly developed?
b. Is there a clear statement of the advantages to be gained from acceptance of the author's proposal?
c. Does the author take the alternatives to his or her proposal into account? Is the author able to demonstrate effectively why these alternative proposals are not acceptable?
d. Does the author deal with opponents or the opposition directly or indirectly? Is he or she fair or unfair in assessing and responding to the opposition?
e. Does the author stick to the issue at hand? Does he or she draw red herrings across the trail or launch into *ad hominem* attack?
f. Does the author acknowledge the problems that go along with, or are created by, his or her proposals? Does the author prove that even with those problems his or her theory is both necessary and more acceptable than any other?
g. Does the author appeal to the reader's emotions or to his or her understanding or to both?
h. Do the examples and details employed in the essay lend sufficient support to the ideas?
i. What authorities does the author call on for support? Is citing evidence from recognized authorities a significant argumentative technique for him or her?
j. Does the use of analogies weaken or strengthen the author's argument?
k. What special techniques, if any, does the author employ to give emphasis to his or her ideas?
l. Has the author done anything to gear discussion to a particular audience? Has the author kept his or her audience in mind in developing the essay rhetorically?

3. How does King defend himself from the charge of being an outside agitator? Is he convincing?

4. Why does King speak of "our legitimate and unavoidable patience"?

5. Central to King's argument is his distinction between just law and unjust law. Ask students to summarize King's distinction, then to discuss it. Do they accept it?

6. Why was King "gravely disappointed with the white moderate"? With the white church and its leadership?

7. What is the effect of language like "prophets," "gospel," "birthright," "millennium," "promise," "devil," "pilgrimage," and "promised land"? In what context does King use it? From what source does it come?

8. Have students choose a particularly striking remark from the "Letter," one they think best represents the piece, and prepare to discuss it in class.

9. Ask students to consider how King's declaration that he stands between the forces of complacency and hatred is at the heart of his essay, in terms of content and in terms of rhetoric. How is King's rhetoric both moderate and moderating?

10. Charles R. Morris devotes some consideration to Martin Luther King, Jr., in his "Civil Disobedience" (NR 785, SE 467). Is he fair/accurate in his treatment of Dr. King?

Suggested Writing Assignments

1. Write an analytical essay in response to Analytical Consideration 10, above.

2. Write an essay in response to King's assertion that "Injustice anywhere is a threat to justice everywhere. We are caught in an inescapable network of mutuality, tied in a single garment of destiny."

3. Write an essay in which you extend by your own example and illustration a definition of the kind of love King refers to and expresses in his letter.

4. Do the experiences related by Maya Angelou in "Graduation" (NR 22, SE 11) and Zora Neale Hurston in "How It Feels to Be Colored Me" (NR 19) in their assertion of personal and racial dignity anticipate King's nonviolent campaign and his "Letter from Birmingham Jail"? Explain.

JAMES THURBER

The Rabbits Who Caused All the Trouble

The Norton Reader, p. 806; Shorter Edition, p. 488

James Thurber's essay should be enjoyable for everyone, though we probably should not take it for granted that students know much about fables, Aesop's fables in particular. Perhaps George Orwell's *Animal Farm* is better known to them. Whatever the case, you might do well to spend some time on this literary genre; you might distribute a few of Aesop's fables and let students work in small groups to come to some understanding of their subject, purpose, and audience. Examples from children's literature could provide useful supplementary material. Robert Scholes makes several useful and applicable points in his *Textual Power* (1985). Two of these could guide classroom work: (1) We read a parable for the story; we interpret it for meaning, and (2) the moral attached by the author may be *a* meaning, but it is not *the* meaning. You might work with these ideas in evaluating "The Rabbits Who Caused All the Trouble" perhaps in comparison with the selections in "Prose Forms: Parables" (NR 1102-1122).

Analytical Considerations

1. What political situation does Thurber present?
2. How would students describe the animal groups presented here?
3. Ask students what textual clues alert them to Thurber's intention to represent a human situation here.
4. Have students analyze the words spoken by the "other animals" and the "wolves." What is the effect of these remarks?
5. Ask students to respond to the wolves' assertion that "This is no world for escapists."
6. Does this fable, written within a political context of more than thirty years ago, have meaning today? Why or why not?
7. How does Thurber use repetition? To what effect?
8. Is the animal fable an effective means of communication? Why? Is it likely to endure?

Suggested Writing Assignments

1. Now that you have read this fable for the story, write an essay in which you interpret it for a meaning or for several meanings.
2. Write an animal fable of your own.
3. Read several of Aesop's fables, and write an essay in which you compare/contrast them with Thurber's. Make rhetorical concerns like subject, purpose, and audience the basis for your comparison/contrast.
4. Write an essay about the meaning of the "Moral." By what process(es) is it arrived at? Does it operate to define or change the meaning and effect of what has gone before?

JONATHAN SWIFT

A Modest Proposal

The Norton Reader, p. 807; Shorter Edition, p. 489

"A Modest Proposal" is often anthologized, for in this essay Jonathan Swift has united a number of rhetorical stratagems which make it not only a brilliant example of sustained irony but a shockingly delightful piece to read. The questions which follow "A Modest Proposal" in the text go a long way toward stimulating comprehension of the essay–especially of Swift's irony.

When we say that "A Modest Proposal" is an essay of sustained irony, we suggest that within it are to be found simultaneously two distinct points of view.* The more obvious point of view, of course, belongs to the speaker, to the proposer himself. His language, his means, and his goals suggest a reasoned concern with an economic problem. The second, and increasingly noticeable, point of view belongs to Swift, who ingeniously calls our attention to ethical and moral matters through the creation of subtle and not so subtle patterns of contrast. As a logical proposition the speaker's "modest proposal" is perhaps supportable. Within the context of human feeling and human morality, as Swift's irony reveals, it is indefensible.

Analytical Considerations

1. Re: content
   a. What is a "projector"?
   b. What is the meaning of "Papist"?
   c. What is to be done with the "poor people who are aged, diseased, or maimed"?
   d. What are "shambles"?
   e. What was the population of Ireland, by the projector's estimate, at the time of "A Modest Proposal"?
2. What situation prompted Swift to write "A Modest Proposal"?
3. Why does the narrator delay announcing his proposal?
4. Prompt students to discover those means (e.g., diction, syntax, sense of evidence) by which the projector creates distance and detachment from the subject.
5. Ask students to describe the persona of the projector.
6. Having arrived at some sense of Swift's subject, students should be asked to define his purpose. Another way to get at that would be to ask students to describe his target.
7. Where is Swift in "A Modest Proposal"? Is he the projector? How do we determine who is who?
8. Encourage students to evaluate "A Modest Proposal" according to the standards of argument (logic, evidence, structure, etc.). What is the projector's argument? What is Swift's argument?
9. For what kind of audience did Swift prepare this satire? Does the satirist have to assume a particular audience before he can write?

*Some of the ideas in this discussion have been adapted from Charles Kay Smith's brilliant analysis of "A Modest Proposal" in *Styles and Structures: Alternative Approaches to College Writing* (New York: W. W. Norton, 1974), pp. 117–38.

Suggested Writing Assignments

1. Read two other satires by Swift, *A Tale of a Tub* and *The Battle of the Books*, and write an essay on "Swift and the Art of Satire."
2. Consider writing an essay about the place and function of satire in contemporary life. Where is it needed? Why?
3. Write a satire of your own on some pressing situation in which a change in policy or some relief is needed. Anticipate probable objections, and address them in your argument.
4. Though it is written ironically, Swift's essay takes up the very real problem of population control, a problem that modern societies have not yet solved. Consider the contemporaneity of Swift's topic, if not his "proposal." Respond to any one of the following questions in an essay:
   a. What is the discernible attitude toward abortion in "A Modest Proposal"? Is it logical to speculate on whether Swift would favor legal abortions or join a right-to-life group were he alive today? How significant have the various birth control methods so far been in limiting population?
   b. Does the problem of how to handle unwanted pregnancies seem as complex in Swift's time as in modern times? Reading "Abortion" by Barbara Grizzuti Harrison (SE 367) may help you answer this question.
   c. Swift's proposals suggest that in a world in which population is increasing and resources are limited, individual liberty must be restrained (voluntarily or legislatively) to some extent. Is a compromise or the willing of personal liberty to the common good one essential basis for a viable social system? Is it part of the American credo?
   d. Do you suppose Swift would side with Betty Rollin ("Motherhood: Who Needs It?" [NR 430, SE 292]) in the essentials of her argument?

Additional questions on this essay will be found in the text (NR 814, SE 496).

NICCOLÒ MACHIAVELLI

The Morals of the Prince

The Norton Reader, p. 815; Shorter Edition, p. 497

Niccolò Machiavelli, the man responsible for the famous dictum "The end justifies the means," has over the centuries been viewed as an agent of all that is diabolical in administrative practices. This reputation was largely established by the chapters in *The Prince* that are reproduced in *The Norton Reader*. Thus, in reading these chapters, one should determine the extent to which they justify Machiavelli's reputation or the connotative meanings of the term "Machiavellian." "The Morals of the Prince" also presents an excellent opportunity to study the mental process we call logic and the rhetorical process we call argumentation.

Analytical Considerations

1. Re: content
   a. Which is better for the prince: to be hated or to be loved?
   b. How is it possible for the prince to be feared, but not hated?
   c. With what did Hannibal hold his army together?
   d. Why must a prince "know how to make good use of both the beast and the man"?
   e. A prince should seem to be imbued with five good qualities; which is the most important of these virtues?
2. Have students select six statements that represent the substance of this section of *The Prince.* Let them be prepared to defend the accuracy and representative quality of their selections.
3. Ask students to describe Machiavelli's sense of human nature.
4. Would students want to live in a state run by a prince or ruler trained according to Machiavelli's principles?
5. This selection could just as well have been placed in the "Ethics" section of the *Reader.* Encourage students to discuss "The Morals of the Prince" from an ethical standpoint. What are Machiavelli's real values as distinguished from those to which he occasionally pays lip service? Is he trustworthy? Honorable?
6. One of the most notable features of Machiavelli's style is his use of the aphorism. Ask students to cull a number from this selection, then to discuss their purpose and effect.
7. How does Machiavelli use examples? What are his customary sources for examples? Why?
8. How does Machiavelli use contrast and repetition?
9. Two important rhetorical concerns merit attention here:
   a. Argument: Each of the four excerpts from *The Prince* is an argument; have students discover the paradigm Machiavelli uses. Is he reasonable or does he merely appear to be reasonable?
   b. Style: Have students analyze this text to uncover the distinct features of Machiavelli's style–e.g., brevity, concision, use of aphoristic syntax. Let them be prepared to write an in-class exercise, say, a 500-word essay, on "Machiavelli's Style."

Suggested Writing Assignments

1. Write an essay on the adjective "Machiavellian" by defining,

illustrating, and applying the term to the world of contemporary politics.

2. Write an essay titled "The End Justifies the Means: Machiavelli's 'The Morals of the Prince.' "

Additional questions on this essay will be found in the text (NR 821, SE 503).

ABRAHAM LINCOLN

Second Inaugural Address

The Norton Reader, p. 822; Shorter Edition, p. 504

Abraham Lincoln's "Second Inaugural Address" should be regarded as a piece of persuasive ceremonial discourse, formal in its tone and diction. Lincoln's persuasive strategy is to move from an objective, rather detached overview of recent events (war is not called war) to a benevolent appeal to the divided nation to accept "God's judgment on North and South" and to work at reunification. Lincoln offers his invitation to the South for reconciliation as something good in and of itself, morally right. In doing so, he makes use of the special rhetorical topic appropriate to ceremonial discourse. He also argues that reconciliation would be advantageous to all, using the special rhetorical topic for deliberative discourse. Toward the end of the "Address," Lincoln refers more and more frequently to God, thus deemphasizing the Civil War in order to encourage reunification of the nation under (and seemingly because of) common religious belief.

Analytical Considerations

1. Ask students to determine the subject, purpose, and audience for the "Second Inaugural Address." Encourage them to work directly and exclusively from the text. Ask, for example, if they could determine the purpose if no title were given. How?

2. What assumptions does Lincoln make about his audience in terms of shared beliefs and values?

3. Though this address reviews history, it is not a mere recitation of events. Why not? Why has Lincoln chosen to speak of only certain events?

4. Analyze Lincoln's diction and syntax. What makes it formal, eloquent, and effective?

5. Lincoln uses three types of rhetorical appeal here: logical, emotional, and ethical. Have students point out where he uses each and to what effect. Which is the most effective? Why?

6. Lincoln's use of repetition is striking here; it may well be the

most effective rhetorical device in the address. Let students circle repeated words and determine how repetition functions (contrast, balance, parallelism, etc.).

Suggested Writing Assignments

1. Write an essay in which you compare/contrast Lincoln's "Second Inaugural Address" with John F. Kennedy's inaugural address in 1961. Be sure to deal with both content and rhetoric.
2. Imagine yourself a member of the loyal opposition to Lincoln, and write a response to his "Second Inaugural Address."
3. Write an essay exploring Lincoln's "Second Inaugural Address" as a cultural document. Research the historical context of Lincoln's second term as president, and use it as a frame for your discussion.

THOMAS JEFFERSON

Original Draft of the Declaration of Independence

The Norton Reader, p. 824; Shorter Edition, p. 506

and

THOMAS JEFFERSON AND OTHERS

The Declaration of Independence

The Norton Reader, p. 828; Shorter Edition, p. 510

The authorship of "The Declaration of Independence" is attributed largely (and quite rightly) to Thomas Jefferson. As the original draft shows, his careful thought, exacting attention to detail, and inspired phrasings determined both the content and much of the expression of the final document. His draft was influenced by several persons, among them Benjamin Franklin and John Adams, and was edited somewhat by members of the Second Continental Congress. But perhaps even more of the revision was done by Thomas Jefferson himself.

The two versions of "The Declaration of Independence" are usefully studied together. Both illustrate a number of rhetorical devices and procedures: assumptions brought to light; defining by ends or means; marshaling evidence based on common consent; drawing conclusions by deduction; repetition and variation; formal diction. But students may take a more important lesson from detailed attention to the improvement of the final version over the original draft. Both versions say about the same things and contain many of the same phrases. The final version, however, contains more direct and simple language than the draft. Also, gratuitous and repetitious phrases have been excised from the final version, and punctuation and spelling have been made consistent.

The two versions of "The Declaration of Independence" thus exemplify the value of editing and revising any piece of writing. Even so insightful and articulate a man as Thomas Jefferson benefits from constructive criticism and careful revision of his work.

Analytical Considerations

1. Ask students to note what remains the same in both versions of "The Declaration of Independence."
2. Then ask them how the final version differs from the draft. This is not just a question of what has been changed but why.
3. Ask students to consider the rhetorical strategy evident in both versions by dividing the text into thirds, labeling those sections by content and function, then describing the rhetorical advantages of the final version over the original draft.
4. Ask students to compare/contrast Jefferson's views on the nature of man, the function of government, and the relationship between morality and political life with those of Niccolò Machiavelli in "The Morals of the Prince" (NR 815, SE 497).
5. In "Is America Falling Apart?" (NR 384, SE 262) Anthony Burgess writes of the "dangerous naiveté of the Declaration of Independence" and characterizes the founding principles of America as "romantic." Does he have any basis for his comments? Whatever his intention in making these remarks, are they necessarily pejorative?
6. Students will discover that Jefferson's last indictment was deleted from the final version. Let them speculate why.

Suggested Writing Assignments

1. From the reading and discussion of the original draft and final version of "The Declaration of Independence," write an essay on the process and function of revision.
2. From your work on these two texts, write an essay on the art of political compromise.
3. Write an essay about what you have learned about Thomas Jefferson from your work on these readings.

Additional questions on this essay will be found in the text (NR 831, SE 513).

E. B. WHITE

Democracy

The Norton Reader, p. 833; Shorter Edition, p. 514

In this short essay, which originally appeared in the *New Yorker*, E. B. White writes on a well-worn topic with wit, precision, and calculated insouciance that make it fresh. Students should realize that this selection is an essay despite its deceptive brevity. White's subject, purpose, and audience are readily discernible; his thesis and the structure of his definition are explicit. White wisely defines "Democracy" using concrete images to which readers will respond emotionally. He neatly avoids pompous abstractions and, we may assume, wonderfully suits the need of a War Board to arouse patriotic fervor.

Analytical Considerations

1. Most definitions have two basic elements–the genus and the differentiae. For example, in the definition of "chair," the class or category "furniture" is the genus, and the detail "in which one person sits" is one of the differentiae, showing how a chair differs from other members of the same genus. What is the genus to which White assigns "democracy"?
2. White creates his definition with a series of impressionistic details.
    a. Can you find a principle by which White has ordered these details? Or are they randomly presented?
    b. Provide examples that demonstrate White's use of repetition and variation in style. How do repetition and variation make for order in White's definition?
3. Examine the first paragraph with students. What does it tell us? How? What are the most salient rhetorical features? How do they create tone and establish White's persona? Are both sustained to the end?
4. An *argumentum ad populum*, using words (often vague abstractions) meant to stir emotions, is sometimes regarded as a fallacious or unfair tactic in arguing a position. Is there anything fallacious in White's definition? Is he being fair? Can you perceive the danger an *argumentum ad populum* may pose when used by a less scrupulous person than White? Explain.
5. Have students explore White's strategies for definition in this piece. How is his choice of metaphor an integral part of the definitions he constructs?
6. Why has White chosen to write about a great abstract like "democracy" by drawing upon so many specifics?

7. You might draw students' attention to the date of composition and ask in what ways "Democracy" is a cultural document.

Comparative Considerations

1. Read at least two other pieces by E. B. White. You may choose from among "Once More to the Lake" (NR 79, SE 53), "Progress and Change" (NR 375, SE 258), and "Some Remarks on Humor" (NR 1076, SE 663). Do you find the characteristics of White's persona described in the above analysis in his other writings? What do you find specifically? Concreteness? Insouciance? Offhandedness? Wit? Humor?

Suggested Writing Assignments

1. Write an essay on what you take to be White's understanding of the responsibilities of the writer in a democracy during wartime.
2. Write a definition of "democracy," using White's strategies but taking details from your own life and times.
3. Defend or refute the validity of White's idea that democracy is "the mustard on the hot dog and the cream in the rationed coffee" or "an idea which hasn't been disproved yet" or "a song the words of which have not gone bad."

Additional questions on this essay will be found in the text (NR 833, SE 514).

SCIENCE

JAMES C. RETTIE

"But a Watch in the Night": A Scientific Fable

Shorter Edition, p. 515

This essay is the only known work by James C. Rettie, who at the time of its writing (1948) was an employee of the National Forest Service. The majority of Rettie's facts are adapted from a government pamphlet on soil erosion. The essay provides us with an interesting example of how statistical information or popularly accepted facts can be tailored for a dramatic effect.

Rettie's essay, a combination of narrative and process analysis put in the service of persuasion, demonstrates the power of extended metaphor. The conceit of the "Copernican film" provides narrative continuity as well as a focal point for the piece. Rettie has written a fable, complete with moral, that enables him to create the distance and objectivity the reader needs to appreciate the viewpoint of the conservationist, which emerges only at the end of the piece.

Analytical Considerations

1. What is the meaning of this fable? Is the moral at the end the only meaning? Why not?
2. Evaluate Rettie's adaptation of the fable form. What is a "scientific fable"?
3. This essay contains a good deal of objective material; ask students if they can discern where Rettie moves from objective to subjective point of view. How can they tell? What is the effect? Is this the point at which he reveals his purpose?
4. You might want to explore Rettie's use of three rhetorical modes here: narrative; exposition (process analysis); and argument (technically persuasion more than argument). The first two are probably much more obvious to students than the last.
5. Does this essay, written forty years ago, retain its significance? Why or why not?

Suggested Writing Assignments

1. Compare " 'But a Watch in the Night' " to another type of modern fable. Look at James Thurber's "The Owl Who Was God" (NR 1123), and analyze the differences and similarities in structure, tone, and purpose between Thurber's fable and Rettie's.
2. Write your own fable on a topic of importance to you.

EDWARD O. WILSON

The Superorganism

The Norton Reader, p. 856; Shorter Edition, p. 520

Edward O. Wilson's essay is a shining example of good scientific writing for lay readers. In describing the behavioral patterns of leafcutter ants in the rain forests of Brazil, Wilson combines a scientist's meticulous observation of detail with a teacher's gift for instructing through analogy. The efficient, harmonious workings of the leafcutter ant colony suggest humankind's need to work toward a more harmonious relationship with the natural world. With fluency and clarity, Wilson documents the process of scientific observation and builds an implicit argument for a strengthened environmental ethic.

Analytical Considerations

1. Re: content
   a. What is the stated purpose of the Amazon project?
   b. What insect was the focus of Wilson's observation?
   c. How are ants guided across a plot of earth?
   d. "No other animals have evolved the ability to turn fresh vegetation into" what?
   e. What accounts for one female ant's becoming queen of a colony?
2. What is the "superorganism"? Why has Wilson labeled it thus?
3. What is the relationship between nature and humankind here? For example, how may we characterize Wilson's relationship with nature? Is he making an implicit argument from example in regard to how we should deal with all the elements of our natural environment?
4. Ask students to describe Wilson's purpose in "The Superorganism." Does he have one great purpose or several purposes? How do students determine a response to this question?
5. How has Wilson structured "The Superorganism"? Why does he take so long to get to the subject of his essay, the leafcutter ants?
6. Ask students what rhetorical features distinguish "The Superorganism." You might direct discussion toward at least three features:
   a. Wilson's narrative fluency
   b. His carefully detailed descriptions, which are often enhanced by superb similes and metaphors (e.g., paragraphs 4, 5, 6, 10, 11, etc.)
   c. The persona he creates in this essay.

Suggested Writing Assignments

1. Wilson quotes Charles Darwin's response to his first encounter with the tropical rain forest near Rio ("wonder, astonishment, & sublime devotion, fill & elevate the mind"). Write an essay on your first response to a sight of great natural beauty.

2. Spend some time observing a process in nature: a cat giving itself a bath; a person falling asleep in the library; a squirrel sequestering a bit of food. Write an essay carefully detailing your observations and offering some summary about that animal's relationship to its world.

3. Do some research on an endangered species or area, and write an essay outlining the problem and proposing a solution.

MICHAEL J. KATZ

On the Wings of an Angel: An Exploration of the Limits of Biological Enterprise

The Norton Reader, p. 866; Shorter Edition, p. 530

This essay might well be called "On Biological Possibilities," for in it Michael J. Katz puts forth a carefully structured and documented argument that "Perhaps, deep within the true province of biology, everything is possible." What at first reading may appear to be a vague generalization takes on persuasive power through Katz's skilled use of the strategies of division, classification, and definition to give coherence to his views. An essential element of Katz's perspective is an understanding of the biologist as an artisan, akin to the literary artisans to whom he refers–Robert Frost, "Sherlock Holmes," and Gertrude Stein.

Analytical Considerations

1. Re: content
   a. What is ontogeny?
   b. What is phylogeny?
   c. How many proteins form the normal clotting cascades in humans?
   d. What is the essential difference between the human eye and that of an octopus?
   e. Why is it that nature cannot create angels' wings?
2. Ask students to state Katz's thesis and means of development.
3. What does Katz mean when he says, "We are all biologists"? What is the role of assertion in his essay?
4. Ask students to consider Katz's meaning in calling the biologist an "artisan."

5. Is Katz careless in his use of the verb "to know" in paragraphs 6 and 7?
6. Ask students to study the introductory paragraphs and the concluding paragraphs. How do these paragraphs function by themselves and in relation to each other?
7. How does Katz use questions in his essay? How does he use repetition?
8. Discuss the significance of the title.

Suggested Writing Assignments

1. Write an essay in which you make a proposal for applying Katz's sense of the limitless possibilities of biology to an urgent contemporary problem.
2. Should there be limits to biological enterprise? If so, how should they be determined and by whom? If no, defend your views against those who might accuse you of endangering lives in the interest of scientific "progress."

KONRAD Z. LORENZ

The Taming of the Shrew

The Norton Reader, p. 879; Shorter Edition, p. 543

Konrad Z. Lorenz's discussion of the characteristics and behavior of the water shrew could have been quite dry and of interest only to the science student–perhaps only to one concerned with insectivores. Instead, there is a genuine and successful attempt to make his subject interesting to the casual reader. Lorenz presents not merely a report of his observations but a narrative of his discovery of the water shrews and his attempts to procure and keep several of them. While the essay does put forward apparently new scientific facts and observations, Lorenz largely avoids scientific jargon and elaborates sufficiently on his observations to make them available to the lay reader. Most significant in attracting general readers, however, is Lorenz's tone in the essay. His diction, his admissions of personal dilemma, and his use of dialogue reflect his excitement about his subject and give the reader a sense of the man behind the study, a sense so often lacking in scientific writing.

Analytical Considerations

1. Re: content
   a. What is a "comparative ethologist"?
   b. On the journey home, what did Lorenz feed his water shrews?

c. How does the fur of the water shrew remain absolutely dry underwater?
d. How have water shrews killed fish more than sixty times their size?
e. Why did the four surviving shrews die?

2. Does Lorenz's approach to scientific observation and experimentation seem classical or innovative, deductive or inductive? What relative weight or emphasis does he give to observation, self-criticism, speculation, and synthesis?

3. Lorenz draws some of his conclusions and records some of his observations of water shrews in terms of analogy with other animals. How is his use of analogy helpful to the lay reader? How is it helpful to the scientist?

4. Do we get to see the *process* of scientific discovery in Lorenz's essay? Have students detail the steps of the discovery process as Lorenz arranges them.

5. In his essay how do the water shrews behave when offered "a large edible frog." What philosophical commentary does Lorenz offer on the episode?

6. Does Jacob Bronowski's "The Reach of Imagination" (NR 194, SE 133) have any relevance to Lorenz's notion of the "creative imagination"?

7. Students are likely to accept Lorenz as an authority and trust his observations and conclusions. To what extent is Lorenz's authority dependent on his use of factual evidence? Or is his authority as much dependent on his ability to engage the reader's interest and sympathy personally? Discuss the role of Lorenz's persona.

8. What is the relevance of the epigraph for the essay?

Suggested Writing Assignments

1. Rewrite Lorenz's report as a simple summary of his experiments and findings. To which of the other essays in the "Science" section is this summary most similar in tone? (Do any of the other essays in the section reveal much about the particular character of the author?)

2. Write an essay in response to this question raised by Konrad Lorenz: "But man should abstain from judging his innocently-cruel fellow creatures, for even if nature sometimes 'shrieks against his creed,' what pain does he himself not inflict upon the living creatures that he hunts for pleasure and not for food?"

Additional questions on this essay will be found in the text (NR 892, SE 556).

STEPHEN JAY GOULD

Our Allotted Lifetimes

The Norton Reader, p. 910; Shorter Edition, p. 556

With characteristic skill in writing for general readers, Stephen Jay Gould's essay shows that the presentation of facts and scientific theory need not be dry and dauntingly abstract. The subject matter of "Our Allotted Lifetimes" is inherently interesting, but even if it were not, it is reinforced so well by the examples and details Gould elects to use in developing it that it would become so. Gould apparently delights in introductions and conclusions. He begins "Our Allotted Lifetimes" outside his real subject. He has recourse to literature in his use of the best seller *Ragtime.* Gould moves cleverly from a fictive discussion of *Ragtime* to his own discussion of mammalian internal time. His conclusion is likewise clever, playing off words and ideas brought up earlier in the essay. Examples throughout his essay are well selected to evoke images and provoke delight. In "Our Allotted Lifetimes" such descriptions as "We marvel at the quickness of a mouse, express boredom at the torpor of a hippopotamus" and such discussions as that of whale songs serve these ends. Gould's presence in the essay--his use of his humor, his informal language, personal pronouns, and personal experience--enhances the essay, making it more than just instructive scientific writing, making it delightful as well.

Analytical Considerations

1. Re: content
   a. What is "scaling theory"?
   b. Among active warm-blooded creatures, which has the slowest heartbeat rhythm?
   c. What is the "price we pay for moving much faster than nature intended"?
   d. The song of what mammal is the "most elaborate single display so far discovered in any animal"?
   e. All mammals, whatever their size, breathe once for how many heartbeats?
2. What examples and details in "Our Allotted Lifetimes" particularly interest you? Discuss their relation to the content of the essay.
3. Does this essay have an explicit or implicit thesis? Ask students to state Gould's thesis.
4. What does Gould mean when he says, "We impose our kitchen clock, ticking equably, upon all things." Is he correct? Give examples.
5. What kinds of evidence does Gould use to support his ideas in "Our Allotted Lifetimes"?

6. What does Gould mean by "absolute time" as opposed to "internal time"? How absolute, in fact, is clock time?

7. Focus students' attention on Gould's introduction and conclusion. Are they effective parts of the essay? Why?

Suggested Writing Assignments

1. Having read Gould's essay, write an explanation of his assertion that "absolute time is not the appropriate measuring stick for all biological phenomena." What would be the advantages and disadvantages of shifting away from an anthropocentric perspective?

2. Read the other selections by Gould in the *Reader* ("Darwin's Middle Road" [NR 945, SE 578] and "The Terrifying Normalcy of AIDS" [NR 643, SE 374]); analyze them carefully; then write a profile of Gould as an essayist.

NIGEL CALDER

Heads and Tails

The Norton Reader, p. 914; Shorter Edition, p. 561

Although this is an essay concerned with defining astronomy, even if in rather quirky terms (as "a four-legged animal standing on sound and false ideas at the front and false observations at the rear"), "Heads and Tails" is more than an essay of definition. It is also a consideration of our misconceptions about our environment and universe. In delightfully witty fashion, Nigel Calder weaves examples of scientific "discoveries" throughout history that shed an ironic but revealing light on our ability or lack of ability to see the world clearly. In relaying the work of his predecessors, Calder avoids condescension. Rather, his conversational, humorous tone enables him to trace some scientific/intellectual history in a most appealing way.

Analytical Considerations

1. Ask students to locate and state Calder's thesis.

2. Discuss the importance of "seeing" in "Heads and Tails." This should be an interesting process of discovery as students realize that nearly every paragraph contains at least one word related to "seeing." Ask them to find and list those words, then to comment on how they function rhetorically and thematically.

3. What is Calder's purpose? For what audience does he write? How do we know?

4. Let students describe, drawing on examples from the text, the persona Calder creates here.

5. What are the "tails of comets"? How does Calder use them as a metaphorical device in his essay?
6. What is Calder's view of what science is and what science does? Compare/contrast his ideas with those of Edward O. Wilson or Stephen Jay Gould or another essayist in the "Science" section of the *Reader.*

Suggested Writing Assignments

1. Investigate one of the figures mentioned by Calder in "Heads and Tails," and write a biographical sketch of 1,000 words or so. You might consider what Virginia Woolf has to say in "The New Biography" (NR 738, SE 420) as you set about this task. Once you have chosen a subject, determine your purpose and audience; have a specific context for publication in mind as well.
2. Using "Heads or Tails" and another essay in the "Science" section, write about the issue of anthropocentrism–interpreting the world in terms of human values–in relation to the natural world.

ARTHUR KOESTLER

Gravity and the Holy Ghost

The Norton Reader, p. 920; Shorter Edition, p. 567

In "Gravity and the Holy Ghost," Arthur Koestler acquaints the general reader with the astronomer Johannes Kepler, whose work prepared for Isaac Newton's more famous theories. The opening observation about their relationship sets up the pattern of development used throughout the essay: cause and effect. Koestler traces Kepler's life and work, showing how one thought or experience led to another. Often the cause-effect relationship seems to work in reverse, a particular effect leading Kepler to insights about causality in a larger matter. This is often the way science works, Koestler would have us know, stating: "The greatness of the philosophers of the scientific revolution consisted not so much in finding the right answers [effects] but in asking the right questions [causes]. . . ."

Analytical Considerations

1. Re: content
   a. What is the subtitle of Kepler's book *A New Astronomy Based on Causation*?
   b. How many laws of planetary motion did Kepler posit?
   c. Who wrote *On the Revolutions of the Heavenly Spheres*?

d. Since the time of Plato, what field of study had been "out of bounds for astronomy"?
e. Kepler's determination of the orbit of what planet became the unifying link between the two formerly separate realms of physics and astronomy?

2. Ask students to determine and explain Koestler's purpose here. For whom does he write?

3. Let students explain what Koestler means when he says that "the mere knowledge that a problem is soluble means that half the game is already won."

4. How is "Gravity and the Holy Ghost" as much an essay on intellectual history as on scientific history?

5. Ask students to explain the meaning and significance of Kepler's replacing a circular orbit with an ovoid orbit. How can a circle be "archetypal"?

6. Is "Gravity and the Holy Ghost" an appropriate title for this essay?

7. Have students contrast Koestler's sense of how scientists work with that of any other writer in the "Science" section, perhaps Michael J. Katz or Jacob Bronowski or Edward O. Wilson.

8. Let students plot the design and means of development used by Koestler in this essay. (They should perceive the central significance of Koestler's use of cause and effect.)

Suggested Writing Assignments

1. Write an essay in response to Koestler's observation that "The greatness of the philosophers of the scientific revolution consisted not so much in finding the right answers but in asking the right questions. . . ." Consider how this comment might have resonances outside the realm of science.

2. Consider Newton's remark "If I have been able to see farther than others, it was because I stood on the shoulders of giants." Write an essay on the significance of Newton's assertion applied to any field of study.

3. Define, in an essay, what Koestler refers to as "inspired cheating." Why is it useful, even necessary, to science?

Additional questions on this essay will be found in the text (NR 926, SE 573).

JACOB BRONOWSKI

The Nature of Scientific Reasoning

The Norton Reader, p. 927; Shorter Edition, p. 574

"The Nature of Scientific Reasoning" is of a piece with Jacob Bronowski's "The Reach of Imagination" (NR 194, SE 133), for both essays express his belief in the imagination as source of discovery in any field of inquiry. Here Bronowski's purpose is to disabuse his readers of the notion that science is a mechanical process of accumulating lifeless facts. He structures his argument around rhetorical questions to get the reader thinking from the start and also to establish a context for the assertions that are the heart of the second half of the essay. Bronowski's ability to define, particularly by means or ends and by negation, and his skill at creating a knowledgeable, trustworthy persona make "The Nature of Scientific Reasoning" effective and instructive, particularly to readers with little scientific knowledge.

Analytical Considerations

1. Crucial to Bronowski's essay is an assertion of importance for all human creativity, whether scientific or artistic: ". . . order must be discovered and, in a deep sense, it must be created." You might want to spend time discussing the meaning and implications of this statement, perhaps in referring to relevant passages from the "Notes on Reading and Writing" (NR xxiii, SE xxi) in the *Reader*, since the same principle informs that essay. Explore why the desire to create order and the search for certainty are fundamental impulses in most human beings. Are these constructive urges? Destructive? Why?
2. What do students see as Bronowski's purpose here?
3. Let students discuss the significance of Bronowski's assertion that "Science finds order and meaning in our experience. . . ." Does this apply to any other disciplines? How?
4. Explain what Bronowski means by saying, "The act of fusion is the creative act."
5. Ask students to consider the significance of Bronowski's assertion that "No scientific theory is a collection of facts." Direct their attention, perhaps, toward rhetoric as well as content, for these two aspects of the essay connect seamlessly in Bronowski's essay. Does this use of assertion establish a pattern for succeeding paragraphs?
6. Ask students if Bronowski's statement that "All science is the search for unity in hidden likenesses" applies to Charles Darwin as presented in Stephen Jay Gould's "Darwin's Middle Road" (NR 945, SE 578), to Johannes Kepler as presented in Arthur Koestler's

"Gravity and the Holy Ghost" (NR 920, SE 567), or to Edward O. Wilson as the narrator in "The Superorganism" (NR 856, SE 520).

7. Bronowski uses a number of questions in the first half of his essay. What kind are they? How does he use them?

8. Should you choose to focus attention on the rhetorical strategy of definition, this essay offers opportunities to study definition by means or ends and definition by negation.

Suggested Writing Assignments

1. Write an essay of comparison/contrast in which you analyze the two essays by Jacob Bronowski in *The Norton Reader.* Can you discern and support with examples characteristic features (tone? persona? strategy?) in Bronowski's essays?

2. "Science finds order and meaning in our experience. . . ." Use examples from your reading or your experience to support or refute Bronowski's assertion.

Additional questions on this essay will be found in the text (NR 930, SE 577).

STEPHEN JAY GOULD

Darwin's Middle Road

The Norton Reader, p. 945; Shorter Edition, p. 578

Stephen Jay Gould typically draws analogies and metaphors from nonscientific sources to forward his views on scientific subjects, especially evolutionary theory. Here he humanizes Charles Darwin, the hero of evolutionists, while still managing to praise him, and in doing so, Gould calls upon Homer, Adam Smith, and Karl Marx for assistance. The *Guide* discussion of "Our Allotted Lifetimes" (page 137) is useful in analyzing Gould's characteristic style.

Analytical Considerations

1. Re: content
   a. Gould opens his essay with an excerpt from what classic literary text?
   b. What is "inductivism"?
   c. Gould maintains that the story of Darwin's observation of what species in the Galápagos Islands needs to be corrected?
   d. Gould believes that the theory of natural selection should be viewed as an extended analogy to the economic theories of _______________.

e. For Gould, what is the "midwife of all creativity"?

2. According to Gould, how did Darwin arrive at the theory of natural selection? What is Darwin's "special contribution" to the understanding of evolution?

3. Examine Gould's discussion of Darwin's reliance on analogy as a creative tool. How does Gould present the concept of natural selection as an extended analogy?

4. What is Gould's purpose here? Where does he give clear expression of his purpose? Is it in a thesis statement? How do the structure and development of his essay reveal his purpose and help achieve it?

5. Since this is in effect an argument, it is necessary to evaluate Gould's evidence. What kinds of evidence does he use? How? What assumptions does he make?

Suggested Writing Assignments

1. Write an essay in response to Gould's observation "The idea of steering a course between undesirable extremes emerges as a central prescription for a sensible life."

2. Write an essay in response to Louis Pasteur's conclusion that fortune favors the prepared mind.

3. Write an essay on the ways in which Gould has modified and adapted some of the traditional ways of thinking about scientists and the work of science. Compare and contrast his understanding with that of any other writer in the "Science" section.

TOM BETHELL

Agnostic Evolutionists

The Norton Reader, p. 952; Shorter Edition, p. 585

Tom Bethell's essay draws the lay reader into the thick of current scientific debate over the validity of Charles Darwin's theory of evolution. The attack on evolution comes not from the expected and much publicized quarter of creationism but from within the realm of science itself, from the "rigorous, scrupulous labelers" of science, the transformed cladists. The transformed cladists are Bethell's agnostic evolutionists. To explain their point of view, Bethell focuses attention on Colin Patterson, a renowned paleontologist specializing in fossil fishes, who, after twenty years of work on evolution, came to the conclusion that Darwin's theory cannot be proved through the fossil record. Bethell leads the reader through both sides of the debate, clearly conveying the complexity and, finally, the irresolvable nature of the controversy. Distorted by inaccurate, dated textbook explanations and a scientific community with little to gain by revealing the limits of evidence, evolution has become a kind of faith, Bethell asserts, not entirely unlike creationism. Portraying the transformed cladists as existential heroes of sorts, "Agnostic Evolutionists" causes the reader to consider issues of scientific "knowledge" and scientific "faith."

Analytical Considerations

1. Re: content
   a. Who is Colin Patterson?
   b. Who is responsible for keeping the public in the dark about in-house arguments on Darwin's theory?
   c. What is a "cladist"? A "transformed cladist"?
   d. What is the "punctuated equilibria" theory of evolution?
   e. For Bethell, what is the "stongest evidence on behalf of evolution"?

2. What is Bethell's position in the debate between the transformed cladists and the evolutionists? Is he only an observer and an investigator? If he has a point of view, how does he convey it? Is he fair in his presentation of evidence and testimony?

3. In what ways is belief in evolution "in large part a matter of faith"? Draw on statements made by scientists in both camps to support your answer.

4. Analyze the use of the language of evolution in the textbook excerpts and interviews included in "Agnostic Evolutionists." Is it a means of clarifying or of obfuscating evolutionary theory? What is the function of the "disguised tautology" Bethell mentions in paragraph 23?

5. On the basis of Bethell's essay, do you see the taxonomists as "bookkeepers and accountants in need of a little loosening up" or as proponents of the "only truly scientific outlook," considering their willingness to live with doubt.

Suggested Writing Assignments

1. Write an essay in which you respond to "Agnostic Evolutionists" from Stephen Jay Gould's point of view.

2. If this essay has caused you to examine–or reexamine–your understanding of science and scientists, write an essay about that process and its results (perhaps a "before" and "after" description and analysis.

3. Write an essay in response to one of Bethell's closing observations: "The human mind, alas, seems on the whole to find such uncertainty intolerable. Most people want certainty in one form (Darwin) or another (the Bible)."

Additional questions on this essay will be found in the text (NR 966, SE 599).

LITERATURE AND THE ARTS

EUDORA WELTY

One Writer's Beginnings

The Norton Reader, p. 976; Shorter Edition, p. 600

Taken from her best-selling memoir of the same title, this essay takes us back to the world of Eudora Welty's childhood in Jackson, Mississippi, and offers an adult's reflections on formative early experience. "One Writer's Beginnings" is clearly a chapter from an intellectual/artistic autobiography. Welty describes the books read to her and the books she read, notes several important texts, and talks about the reading process. But the most important aspect of "One Writer's Beginnings" comes near the end when Welty considers "voice." Her six-paragraph treatment of the subject, beginning with her mother's songs and records played on the Victrola, then retracing her own reading and writing experience, provides a valuable opportunity to define and illustrate this difficult rhetorical concept.

Analytical Considerations

1. Re: content
   a. Where was the "library" in Welty's home?
   b. Identify" *Our Wonder World.*
   c. Welty's fascination with the alphabet culminated in her seeing what famous manuscript?
   d. With what word as illustration does Welty describe her "physical awareness of the word"?
   e. How does Welty define the "voice of the story"?

2. Ask students why this selection has been titled "One Writer's Beginnings."

2. Welty says, "Movement must be at the very heart of listening." This is also true for reading. Ask students to plot the movement of "One Writer's Beginnings." Then have them consider what unifies the piece.

4. Ask students to consider the ways in which this is a cultural document reflecting the world of the American South in the early decades of this century.

5. Direct students' attention to the opening paragraph. Ask them to comment on its effect(s). How does it function? What elements make it successful? Have a student read the opening paragraph aloud, drawing attention to Welty's use of alliteration to give the opening rhythm and movement.

6. Welty makes a simple but incisive comment about children, animals, and artists (paragraph 17), a remark worth asking students to discuss by drawing upon examples from painting, sculpture, dance, and music as well as from writing.

7. What do students make of Welty's discussion of her "physical awareness of the word"? Have they had similar experiences? About what words?

8. In paragraph 24 Welty offers a marvelous description of "voice" in a story or poem. After discussing it, ask students to characterize the voice they hear in "One Writer's Beginnings."

Suggested Writing Assignments

1. In describing her reading of classic tales from *Every Child's Story Book*, Eudora Welty notes: "I located myself in these pages and could go straight to the stories and pictures I loved." If you have had the same experience, write an essay about it.

2. "Learning stamps you with its moments. Childhood's learning is made up of moments. It isn't steady. It's a pulse." Reflect on your own educational experience, both formal and informal; then write an essay in response to Welty's observations.

3. Turn your response to Analytical Consideration 6 above into an essay on "The Vision of the Artist."

Additional questions on this essay will be found in the text (NR 982, SE 606).

JOHN GARDNER

What Writers Do

The Norton Reader, p. 982; Shorter Edition, p. 606

"What Writers Do" is an extraordinary and exhaustive exercise in definition. John Gardner, novelist and noted scholar of Chaucer, opens with a succinct, seemingly circular definition that "fiction writers write fiction" and then proceeds to clarify this statement by carefully defining each component contained therein. Drawing on a wide range of examples and metaphors, Gardner writes for a well-read audience, but the principles of his discussion are available to a broader audience.

Analytical Considerations

1. Re: content
   a. Name one of the two "greatest writers" mentioned in "What Writers Do."

b. How many cows had to be killed to make a Bible?
c. What was William Faulkner's genius?
d. For Gardner, what writer "carried most of twentieth-century fiction with him"?
e. What is "mimesis"?

2. Do students agree with Gardner's definition of a great writer? ("A great writer is not great because he never writes dirty limericks but because, if he does write one, he tries to write a very good one.")

3. Does it make sense to describe the writer's mind as "a noble democracy," as Gardner does in paragraph 4?

4. For what audience does Gardner write? What textual clues enable the reader to gain a sense of his audience?

5. How does Gardner distinguish "great children's literature" from "bad children's literature"? Why does he use children's literature to illustrate his point?

6. How does Gardner define "trash" fiction?

7. Have students consider and be prepared to discuss in class the following statements from "What Writers Do":

a. "Indeed, the first-draft stupidity of great writers is a shocking and comforting thing to see."
b. "For artists, writing has always meant, in effect, the art of endless revising."
c. "The true writer sets up for us some important question, in dramatic form, and explores it clear-mindedly, relentlessly."

8. What is a "shining performance" for Gardner?

9. How do students respond to Gardner's theory of art? Do they accept this moral sense of art and the artist?

10. Ask students to evaluate Gardner's definition of "a true work of fiction." Can they suggest works that merit this distinction?

Suggested Writing Assignments

1. Write an argument for or against Gardner's assertion that "The only conceivable reason for engaging in writing is to make something relatively permanent which one might otherwise forget."

2. Gardner attributes considerable importance to revision as part of the composing process. On the basis of his understanding and your own experience, write an essay on "The Art of Revision."

NORTHROP FRYE

The Motive for Metaphor

The Norton Reader, p. 997; Shorter Edition, p. 616

In this essay intended for students and critics of literature, Northrop Frye explores and classifies elements of the human mind as he develops a theory of creative language. His own use of metaphor and analogy makes this a sort of metareflection. His ability to pose resonant questions (e.g., in regard to the social value of literature, the identity of the poet) and suggest possible responses distinguishes this essay, which finds the roots of imagination in our desires and powers of synthesis.

Analytical Considerations

1. What is the "motive for metaphor"?
2. What are the three levels of the mind? How does each operate? Why does Frye take such pains to distinguish them?
3. In paragraph 5 Frye presents his understanding of how science works. Compare/contrast that with the understanding of Jacob Bronowski in "The Nature of Scientific Reasoning" (NR 927, SE 574) or Stephen Jay Gould in "Darwin's Middle Road" (NR 945, SE 578).
4. How does Frye distinguish the arts from the sciences? Do students accept his distinctions?
5. Why does Frye devote a substantial paragraph to his understanding that "Literature doesn't evolve or improve or progress"?
6. What is the students' response to Frye's question "Is it possible that literature, especially poetry, is something that a scientific civilization like ours will eventually outgrow?"
7. Important to this essay is the extended analogy of shipwrecked existence. In the last paragraph Frye notes that "analogy, or likeness to something else, is very tricky to handle in description, because the differences are as important as the resemblances." Has Frye himself succeeded or failed here?
8. Are metaphors lies?
9. How does Frye use questions, particularly in the opening paragraph? Where else does he use them? How? Compare/contrast his use with that of Bronowski in "The Nature of Scientific Reasoning."
10. Have students plot the design of this essay, accounting for organization, development, direction, and points of emphasis. The concluding paragraph merits consideration as well.
11. Discuss John Gardner and Northrop Frye in the role of imagination and the purpose of literary art.

Suggested Writing Assignments

1. Write an essay about Frye's assertion that "the simplest questions are not only the hardest to answer, but the most important to ask. . . ."
2. Write an essay comparing/contrasting Frye and Jacob

Bronowski ("The Reach of Imagination" [NR 194, SE 133]) on imagination.

Additional questions on this essay will be found in the text (NR 1005, SE 624).

CARL GUSTAV JUNG

The Poet

The Norton Reader, p. 1021; Shorter Edition, p. 625

It is commonplace that "history repeats itself," and we all have at one time or another been able to identify sympathetically with the situations of other people because we have had related experiences. The psychoanalyst Carl Jung went beyond (or deeper than) the commonplace, however, in perceiving a pattern of wholeness in human existence. Jung observed that certain images and myths recur in the dreams and literatures of peoples separated by vast spatial and temporal distances. From such observations Jung extrapolated his theory of the collective unconscious, in which he articulated the belief that individuals share or "participate" unconsciously in a culture that embraces the whole past experiences of humankind and that thus all human beings are psychically linked.

In this essay Jung's objective is to define the poet (or artist) by elucidating his or her role in the collective life of humanity. It is the poet who articulates the symbols or "archetypes" of felt human experience inherent in all of us. As he does so, he is impersonal in the sense that he is generic man speaking "to the spirit and heart of mankind." It is from this vantage point that we can understand Jung's crucial distinction between the poet as personality and the poet as creator (the poet qua poet), and how "it is not Goethe who creates *Faust*, but *Faust* which creates Goethe."

Analytical Considerations

1. Crucial to accepting Jung's understanding of the poet is his assumption of a distinction between the "artist as person" and the "man as artist." Does he develop and support this debatable proposition in convincing fashion?
2. Ask students what they think of Jung's definition of art in paragraph 3: "Art is a kind of innate drive that seizes a human being and makes him its instrument."
3. What assumptions does Jung make concerning art and the artist?
4. Ask students to describe Jung's persona here. What is its most

prominent feature? Whence comes the authority of a psychiatrist to discourse on poetry? Is it earned or simply assumed?

5. What is the effect of the first sentence of "The Poet"? Are the expectations raised fulfilled in the course of the essay? Where? How? Why?

6. In speaking about the artist, Jung notes that "his own work outgrows him as a child its mother." This may be worth exploring in reference to particular "great works," say, a play by Shakespeare that most students have read.

7. Ask students to consider Jung's use of metaphor in relation to Frye's discussion of its significance in "The Motive for Metaphor" (NR 997, SE 616).

8. Have students cull several debatable assertions from "The Poet." Classify the assertions (generalizations? unqualified assumptions?); then discuss them. Why and how does Jung use such statements? Among others, the following certainly merit scrutiny:

   a. "The creative process has feminine quality."
   b. "It is not Goethe who creates *Faust*, but *Faust* which creates Goethe."
   c. "Both play upon something that reverberates in the Germanic soul. . . ."

9. Is it true that "every great work of art . . . profoundly moves us each and all"?

10. In the end, has Jung been able to "explain the poet"?

Suggested Writing Assignments

1. Write an argument for or against Jung's assertion that "When a form of 'art' is primarily personal it deserves to be treated as if it were a neurosis."

2. Respond to Jung's comment that "A great work of art is like a dream . . ." by relating it to specific works.

3. Write your own essay entitled "The Poet."

Additional questions on this essay will be found in the text (NR 1025, SE 629).

ROBERT FROST

Education by Poetry: A Meditative Monologue

The Norton Reader, p. 1026; Shorter Edition, p. 630

Robert Frost's rather personal and quirky address to Amherst students in 1930 will acquaint students with one of twentieth-century America's most famous writers, whose poetry they may have sampled but who looms as a literary figure rather than as a distinct personality. "Education by Poetry" should remedy that, for here Frost reveals much about himself not only by what he says but by his means of saying it. The poet presents himself as a teacher and, in the course of developing his thoughts on the nature and function of poetic metaphor, interjects his views on the role of colleges in imparting "taste and judgment" and on the ability to discern metaphor in the world beyond poetry–in science, philosophy, history, psychology. In a voice both humorous and cantankerous, Frost takes his students on a circuitous route to the understanding that poetry teaches metaphor, that metaphor leads to belief–in self, love, country, God–and that belief is the only means of bringing something into being, of living creatively and responsively. By Frost's oddly rambling, oddly unified reasoning, poetry is the basis of life.

Analytical Considerations

1. Explain Frost's thesis: "Education by poetry is education by metaphor."
2. Ask students to clarify the ways in which Frost understands metaphor.
3. For Frost, what is the "connection between thought and metaphor"?
4. What does Frost mean when he says, "To learn to write is to learn to have ideas"?
5. Why does Frost not offer his reader examples of the metaphors "to live by"?
6. Why does Frost explore the several dimensions of the word "belief"?
7. Compare/contrast Frost and Carl Gustav Jung on the poet's task.
8. In what ways do Frost and Northrop Frye agree/disagree on the meaning and function of metaphor?
9. In perhaps a dozen places Frost digresses or becomes parenthetic. Are these digression distractions or effective rhetorical devices that contribute to his purpose?
10. What are the effects of Frost's opening paragraphs?
11. Ask students to determine if there is order or a pattern to this essay. If so, what provides the thread of continuity? Is it persona? Theme? Imagery?
12. Where and how does Frost use the techniques of definition in "Education by Poetry"?
13. "Education by Poetry" is a speech. How is an oral performance different from a written presentation? If you had the chance to work with Frost and prepare this speech for publication, what changes would you suggest? Why?

Suggested Writing Assignments

1. The Latin poet Horace said that poetry should both delight and teach. Would Frost agree? Moreover, does Frost do this in his prose as well as in his poetry? Write a careful, analytical essay on the subject.
2. Write an essay on what poetry and poets mean to you.
3. Write an essay in response to Frost's declaration "We ask people to think, and we don't show them what thinking is."
4. Write an essay in which you defend or attack Frost's noting that "The canvas is where the work of art is, where we make the conquest."

Additional questions on this essay will be found in the text (NR 1034, SE 638).

MARGARET ATWOOD

Writing the Male Character

The Norton Reader, p. 1042; Shorter Edition, p. 639

This is a bright, witty, and intensely personal statement on issues of literary art and sexual perspective. Originally delivered as a lecture, "Writing the Male Character" reveals Margaret Atwood's characteristic style–learned, discursive, and occasionally antagonistic–as well as some of her substance. Atwood's concerns about her roles as woman and writer merge here, enabling her to craft a moving declaration of conviction. Students may have difficulty in discerning that this is an argument. Because it is an argument presented in somewhat different fashion, you may need to spend considerable time demonstrating Atwood's technique.

Analytical Considerations

1. Have students summarize Atwood's argument. What is her thesis? How does she structure her argument? What does she use for evidence? Is she convincing?
2. If students accept Atwood's assertion that men and women "*don't think the same*, except about things like higher math," what do they feel accounts for the difference: "natural" factors or socio-cultural conditioning?
3. How important is Atwood's parenthetic playing with the phrase "a male friend of mine" (paragraph 10)?
4. Is the "digression" about Henri Fabre really a digression?
5. Have a student prepare to read paragraphs 2 and 3 aloud. Afterward direct discussion to a consideration of Atwood's tone and

the means by which she achieves it here and at other points in "Writing the Male Character." Does her tone enhance her argument?

6. Atwood uses the device of comparison/contrast (particularly contrast) repeatedly. Let students point out several examples, then discuss each in and for itself and as part of the design of the essay.

7. How does Atwood distinguish the novelist from the critic?

8. Have students draw up a list of the points Atwood wishes to establish here. What is her agenda?

9. What is Atwood's purpose?

Suggested Writing Assignments

1. Write an essay in response to Atwood's assertion that "one cannot deprive any part of humanity of the definition 'human' without grievous risk to one's own soul."

2. Atwood relays her friend's essential criterion for evaluating literature ("Does it live or does it die?"). Think about several books you have read; then evaluate one or all of them according to this standard. Do you think it is a rewarding way to consider literature?

3. Near the end of her essay Atwood notes, "If writing novels—and reading them—have any redeeming social value, it's probably that they force you to imagine what it's like to be somebody else." If you have read a novel that has done that for you, write an essay about the meaning and consequences of that experience.

Additional questions on this essay will be found in the text (NR 1052, SE 649).

VIRGINIA WOOLF

In Search of a Room of One's Own

The Norton Reader, p. 1053; Shorter Edition, p. 650

This essay is Chapter 3 of Virginia Woolf's *A Room of One's Own*, a central document in twentieth-century feminist criticism and scholarship. The work began as two lectures given to undergraduates at two of Cambridge University's women's colleges, Girton and Newnham, in 1928. Woolf then developed the lectures into a text. "In Search of a Room of One's Own" presents Woolf at her characteristic best: impassioned, witty, learned, and insightful. The essay operates on the historical, imaginative, and personal levels simultaneously, for Woolf writes about the plight of women writers in history—emblematized by the fictitious Judith Shakespeare—which leads to expression of her own concern that any woman who would write find the means and space to work undistractedly. Her essay gives splendid illustration to the principles of the "new biography," which she sets forth in an essay of the same title found in *The Norton Reader* (NR 738, SE 420).

Analytical Considerations

1. Re: content
   a. Who wrote the *History of England* to which Woolf refers in the opening of her essay?
   b. What discovery led Woolf to write this essay?
   c. Who was Judith Shakespeare?
   d. Who was Mr. Oscar Browning?
   e. What made Shakespeare's mind "incandescent"?
2. Why has Woolf chosen to limit her consideration to the living conditions of women in England during the time of Elizabeth?
3. Explain what Woolf means when she says that "fiction is like a spider's web, attached ever so lightly perhaps, but still attached to life at all four corners."
4. What, according to Woolf, is the image of womanhood gained from studying poetry and fiction written by men. Do you agree with her assessment?
5. What does Woolf mean by saying, "It is one of the great advantages of being a woman that one can pass even a very fine negress without wishing to make an Englishwoman of her"?
6. How does Woolf answer the question she poses: What is the state of mind that is most propitious to the act of creation?
7. Let students focus on the last seven sentences of paragraph 6 (about the bishop), and analyze what each sentence does. What is the total effect of the passage? How does Woolf use the bishop again? Does he become a metaphor for her in this essay?
8. In what ways is this a cultural document?
9. In what ways is this a personal statement?
10. What is Woolf's purpose here? How do we know?
11. Do Frances FitzGerald ("Rewriting American History" [NR 744, SE 426]) and Woolf share concerns and strategies?

Comparative Considerations

This essay is quite clearly a lecture marked by the demands and conventions of spoken performance. After discerning those textual clues and strategies which characterize the piece as a lecture, turn to other essays by Woolf in *The Norton Reader*, all of them written for publication, not for oral delivery, and let students study them for the ways in which Woolf adapts her technique and style for an audience of readers rather than listeners. Direct the reading and discussion toward the preparation of an essay on the subject.

Suggested Writing Assignments

1. Write an essay evaluating the success or failure of Woolf's arguments as put forth in "In Search of a Room of One's Own."
2. Write an essay in response to Woolf's description of "that very interesting and obscure masculine complex . . . ; that deep-seated desire, not so much that *she* shall be inferior as that *he* shall be superior. . . ."
3. "Unimpeded" is a key word in Woolf's essay. Discuss what the term represents in political, physical, and psychological terms for the artists–men, women, or both–whom Woolf discusses.

S. I. HAYAKAWA

Sex Is Not a Spectator Sport

The Norton Reader, p. 1064; Shorter Edition, p. 661

S. I. Hayakawa's essay is a tightly constructed argument bound to generate lively discussion and writing. His argument is clear and cogent; his tone, crisp and emphatic. "Sex Is Not a Spectator Sport" bears careful scrutiny, however, for Hayakawa's rhetorical skill can overpower the reader into an uncritical acceptance of his assumptions, definitions, and analogies. Since Hayakawa's argument hinges on his definitions of "pornography" and "obscenity," you might consider prefacing the assignment of this essay with a short in-class discussion of the terms, then ask students to read the essay, analyze Hayakawa's definitions, and compare them with definitions from other sources for class discussion.

Analytical Considerations

1. Ask students why they think Hayakawa begins his second paragraph by prefacing his first sentence with "What I am saying."
2. Do students agree with Hayakawa's assertion that "obscenity and pornography can happen only when sexual events are seen from the outside, from a spectator's point of view"?
3. Let students summarize Hayakawa's argument? Is it convincing? Why or why not?
4. Hayakawa's reference to Dante's *Divine Comedy* provides an opportunity to explore the dimension of silence. What is the power of the unsaid? Why can suggestion sometimes be more powerful than explicit statement?
5. Have students analyze the means by which Hayakawa develops his paragraphs (paragraphs 3, 4, and 5 may be particularly appropriate).

6. Ask students to describe the persona Hayakawa creates here. Is it fair, honest, knowledgeable, and trustworthy?
7. Ask students what they would consider a suitable context for the publication of "Sex Is Not a Spectator Sport." Why?

Suggested Writing Assignments

1. Write an essay on Hayakawa's assertion "To concentrate on the mechanics of sex is to ignore altogether its human significance."
2. In the last paragraph of his essay Hayakawa presents two responses to showing movies such as those he lists. Choose a side in the debate, and write an argument to support your position.

Additional questions on this essay will be found in the text (NR 1065, SE 662).

E. B. WHITE

Some Remarks on Humor

The Norton Reader, p. 1076; Shorter Edition, p. 663

Ostensibly offhand in its title and its content, "Some Remarks on Humor" offers the reader a penetrating piece on the difficulties of defining. E. B. White's deliberate avoidance of a precise definition of the term "humor" underscores his remark that "Essentially, it [humor] is a complete mystery." As with other selections by White, this piece can be profitably analyzed to comprehend better how a natural and engaging persona is established.

Analytical Considerations

1. Why is it impossible to define "humor"? Why has White used metaphor and analogy?
2. Ask students to locate White's thesis.
3. Has White succeeded in creating a definition for "humor" or merely offered a description?
4. Have students read several "humorous" pieces in the *Reader*, perhaps those by James Thurber or Ian Frazier or Garrison Keillor or S. J. Perelman, and analyze them as humor according to White's understanding of the term.
5. Ask students to explain how and why White compares humor and poetry in the last paragraph.
6. Have students develop a profile of White as a stylist by drawing up a list of rhetorical features that distinguish his prose.

Comparative Considerations

1. Compare "Some Remarks on Humor" with "Democracy" (NR 833, SE 514) as exercises in using metaphor and analogy to describe, rather than define, a term.

2. Compare "Some Remarks on Humor" with the other three selections by White. Ask students if they can discern distinguishing features of White's style. Characteristic rhetorical strategies? A recognizable persona? After discussion, ask them to turn their reflections into an essay that attempts to answer a question: Why is White considered a master of the informal essay?

Suggested Writing Assignments

1. If White has set you thinking about the subject, define "humor" in an essay of your own. You might consider using several strategies for definition, particularly example. Avoid lexical definitions.

2. Write an essay on the place of humor in contemporary life. Is it necessary? Should some kinds be avoided?

3. Consider writing an essay on humor as it is used by a well-known columnist, television commentator, or political satirist. Study several of her/his pieces; then write an essay of analysis and evaluation.

Additional questions on this essay will be found in the text (NR 1077, SE 664).

X. J. KENNEDY

Who Killed King Kong?

Shorter Edition, p. 664

X. J. Kennedy's answer to his question "Who Killed King Kong?" leads to an intriguing explanation of the lasting appeal of the B-grade movie *King Kong*, as well as to insight into the psychology of the individual in modern technological society.

King Kong represents one aspect of human nature—the instinctive, untamed side that finds itself increasingly at variance with a world run on, and even built by, machines. It is as Kong rails at the world, smashing airplanes and commuter trains in short-lived triumph, that he strikes a responsive chord in us. Kennedy makes this point explicitly. But there is certainly another side to human nature—the side represented by Fay Wray, the Dartmouth hero, the Army Air Corps. It is ironic that the world in which we may feel uncomfortable, and which we may occasionally wish to smash, is of our own making; it stems from our possibly misguided endeavor to progress away from the "ape in us." Kong's opponents, then, are the forces of civilization that built bigger and better machines and now may be subordinate to those machines.

The movie *King Kong* remains fascinating, Kennedy would have us know, because it depicts a compelling modern irony. In the "jungle built by machines," we are passive spectators, only vicariously able to swing in (and out at) that jungle. As we sit passively watching while a mechanical culture perpetuates itself, we tacitly condone the killing of the King Kong aspect in ourselves.

Analytical Considerations

1. Does Kennedy answer the question he poses in the title? Where? How?
2. "Who Killed King Kong?" is very much a cultural document. Ask students to list the references that establish a particular cultural context for the essay. After discussing them, they should consider whether or not this essay is dated. Does its value transcend time?
3. Why do you suppose "Who Killed King Kong?" appears in the "Literature and the Arts" section of *The Norton Reader*? Is it merely because *King Kong* is a film and hence one of the "Arts"?
4. Some consideration of Kennedy's rhetorical method could be profitable. Have students analyze the opening paragraphs. What is Kennedy doing by discussing the continuing popularity of the movie? By exploring the reasons for the widespread appeal of *King Kong* before finally responding to the title question in paragraph 10?
5. Does Kennedy "overread" or "misread" in his discussion of the film's popularity in the South (paragraph 11)? What does it tell the reader about the author?
6. What is Kennedy's tone? How does it contribute to the development of a distinctive persona here?
7. Kennedy's essay probes two sides of the human person: the natural and instinctive element shown by King Kong and the ordered, "civilized" side shown by Fay Wray, the Dartmouth hero, and the Army Air Corps. How do we reconcile these two dimensions? Have we created outlets in modern society to release the animal element? What might they be? Are they effective in purging the "ape within"?
8. What makes watching *King Kong* or any horror film a frightening experience: the external images of horror on the screen or the sense that those images reflect some aspect of our own nature?
9. Does a B-grade movie like *King Kong* qualify as art?

Suggested Writing Assignments

1. Write an analysis of a movie you know well, and attempt to show how it points up aspects of contemporary culture.
2. Write an argument for or against the notion that the individual in modern society is a victim of the very machines created to improve the quality of life.

AARON COPLAND

How We Listen

The Norton Reader, p. 1078; Shorter Edition, p. 668

Aaron Copland, long one of America's best-loved composers, writes a clear and cogent analysis of the listening process in "How We Listen." In explaining the basic concepts of music appreciation, Copland's essay neatly illustrates the rhetorical principles of analysis and synthesis. Because of Copland's evident wish to be informative and instructive, he takes great pains to be clear. The design of his essay, the use of example and analogy, and the simplicity of language and syntax help accomplish his purpose, leading us to the conclusion that we listen to music on several different levels of appreciation at the same time.

Analytical Considerations

1. Why do we "find Tchaikovsky easier to 'understand' than Beethoven"?
2. Does Copland give us his criteria for determining who is the "greater" composer, Ravel or Beethoven?
3. Why does Copland oppose attempts to pin "a meaning-word" on music?
4. Have students plot the design of this essay, annotating each paragraph to show how it functions within the scheme of the whole.
5. How well does Copland use classification to develop "How We Listen"? Are his categories mutually exclusive and clearly explained?
6. How does Copland use analogy? Is it effective? Necessary?
7. What do students make of Copland's references to "simple-minded souls" and the "man in the street" or "One timid lady"?

Suggested Writing Assignments

1. The author mentions the "subjective and objective attitude" necessary to musical composition. Write an essay analyzing his categories of listening as a subjective or objective process.
2. Does Copland make any judgments or imply any judgment that

would indicate that he considers one "plane" of appreciation more worthwhile than others? Explain.

3. Write a rhetorical analysis of "How We Listen," carefully documenting the means by which Copland succeeds or fails in discussing a difficult topic.

4. Apply the categories of listening discussed in Copland's essay to a piece of his own music. Consider an example which has a theme.

JOAN DIDION

Georgia O'Keeffe

The Norton Reader, p. 1098; Shorter Edition, p. 673

This brief and fluent essay on an artist long considered an American original is distinguished by a style of stunning clarity. In crafting a "biostatement" about the painter, Joan Didion has done more than present the quintessential O'Keeffe. She has raised discussion to the level of several great abstracts (style, identity, creativity, and sexuality) while efficiently integrating herself, her daughter, and her reader into the narrative text.

Analytical Considerations

1. Summarize Didion's purpose in "Georgia O'Keeffe." Is her thesis implicit or explicit?

2. What is the effect of the opening paragraph with its weaving together of artist and mother and child?

3. How can a painting be "astonishingly aggressive"?

4. Georgia O'Keeffe's remark to "those city men who stood accused of sentimentalizing her flowers" (paragraph 4) cuts to the heart of a particular kind of criticism. You might want to use this as a way of discussing the nature and function of criticism. Is the subjective an unavoidable element of any criticism?

5. "Style is character," Didion tells us. Ask students to deduce her character from "Georgia O'Keeffe." Can style be used in an immoral and deceptive way?

6. Where and how does Didion use repetition?

7. Ask students why Didion saves most of the standard biographical data until the end of her essay.

8. Have students consider the last three sentences of this essay for voice, effect, and rhythm as well as content. What makes Didion's conclusion resonant and effective?

Suggested Writing Assignments

1. Write an essay on the appeal of Georgia O'Keeffe as a person and as an artist. It might be a good idea to do some research on the subject.
2. Write an essay analyzing Didion's prose style in "Georgia O'Keeffe" and evaluating her success as an essayist.

PHILOSOPHY AND RELIGION

E. F. SCHUMACHER

Levels of Being

The Norton Reader, p. 1129; Shorter Edition, p. 677

With painstaking clarity and care, E. F. Schumacher exhorts his readers to realize the powers of self-awareness and "powers higher than self-awareness" available only to human beings. In this carefully reasoned essay of definition and classification, Schumacher establishes a hierarchy of matter and life, built on the traditional Chain of Being metaphor, which he explains both in words and in symbols as a means of reinforcing his point. In spite of Schumacher's emphatic assertion that the four great levels of being characterized by their elements–matter, life, consciousness, and self-awareness–are "irreducible mysteries," on close analysis the reader recognizes that Schumacher's system rests on disputable boundaries and assumptions, particularly in the distinctions it draws between consciousness and self-awareness. Though his tone is that of a logician, his language on occasion that of a scientist (note the use of mathematical variable, the "elements" of each level of being), Schumacher's aim is that of a metaphysician leading his readers toward reflection and contemplation.

Analytical Considerations

1. What are the "levels of being"?
2. What is "ontological discontinuity"?
3. Several passages might serve as catalysts for discussion, among them:
    a. "Evolution as a process of the spontaneous, accidental emergence of the powers of life, consciousness, and self-awareness, out of inanimate matter, is totally incomprehensible."
    b. "The extraordinary thing about the modern life sciences" is that they hardly ever deal with *life as such*, the factor *x*, but devote infinite attention to the study and analysis of the physiochemical body that is life's carrier. It may well be that modern science has no method for coming to grips with *life as such*. If this is so, let it be frankly admitted; there is no excuse for the pretense that life is nothing but physics and chemistry."
    c. "Nothing is more conducive to the brutalization of the modern world than the launching, in the name of science, of

wrongful and degrading definitions of man, such as 'the naked ape.' "

4. For Schumacher, what is the difference between "consciousness" and "self-awareness"?

5. For Schumacher, what is a "three-dimensional being"?

6. What does Schumacher mean by calling a word label "a finger pointing to the moon"?

7. How does repetition function as rhetorical strategy in "Levels of Being"? What does Schumacher's use of symbolic letters and equations contribute to the essay?

8. Ask students to evaluate Schumacher's concluding paragraph. How does it turn inward and outward, backward and forward, and reveal what may be his most important purpose here?

Suggested Writing Assignments

1. Write an essay in response to Schumacher's assertion that "Nothing is more conducive to the brutalization of the modern world than the launching, in the name of science, of wrongful and degrading definitions of man, such as 'the naked ape.' "

2. Write an essay in response to the remarks of Catherine Roberts, cited by Schumacher in paragraph 19 of his essay.

3. Schumacher refers to the "shadowy existence" of animals since they live in only two dimensions of being–life and consciousness. Using the shadow metaphor as your starting point, write an essay comparing Schumacher's thinking in "Levels of Being" with Plato's "Allegory of the Cave" (NR 1105, SE 685).

PLATO

The Allegory of the Cave

The Norton Reader, p. 1105; Shorter Edition, p. 685

"The Allegory of the Cave" comes from Plato's great treatise on politics and government the *Republic.* In it Plato, using his teacher Socrates as his mouthpiece, instructs Glaucon on the subject of human knowledge. Chained in an underground den, the cave dwellers see only their shadows on the wall, cast by the fire behind them. The shadows that only suggest the pure forms that exist in the realm of ideas, constitute the reality of the cave dwellers. By training the mind to contemplate the pure forms, the cave dwellers can struggle into the sunlit world of ideas above.

Plato's use of the literary form of allegory and his characteristic use of the Socratic dialogue will require some explanation and discussion. You might consider doing a rhetorical unit on allegory, working with allegorical writing by Aesop, James Thurber, and

George Orwell, since the tradition presents opportunities to consider reading as a process for creating meaning at an accessible level.

Analytical Considerations

1. What is Socrates trying to teach Glaucon in "The Allegory of the Cave"? Is it a lesson about abstract qualities?
2. This allegory may be read as a discussion of appearance and reality; as such, it deals with long-standing polarities. Why are human beings sometimes distrustful of appearances?
3. Are there people who "entertain these false notions and live in this miserable manner" today?
4. Do students accept the conclusion set forth in the last line?
5. Socrates offers his own interpretation of the allegory, but it is one among a number of others. What is it meant to represent? What does it represent? How do we know?
6. Ask students to comment on how imagery connected with sight and light works here. Are these clusters stylistic devices? Do they have metaphoric importance?
7. About whom might Socrates be talking in the paragraph that begins "Moreover, I said, you must not wonder"?
8. Ask students to describe the features of a Socratic dialogue. What is the role of "instructor"? Student? Do they think it is an effective means of teaching?
9. How do we know that Plato, not Socrates, wrote this?
10. Does this allegory, now more than twenty-five centuries old, have anything to do with readers today?

Suggested Writing Assignments

1. Since meaning emerges only when you read–and often write about–a text, write an essay in which you interpret "The Allegory of the Cave" by offering a reading of your own.
2. Write an essay setting forth the advantages and disadvantages of applying the Socratic method to undergraduate education today.
3. Do some research on Plato and Socrates. Then write a 750-word essay that might serve as an introduction to "The Allegory of the Cave" in *The Norton Reader.*

PAUL TILLICH

The Riddle of Inequality

The Norton Reader, p. 1147; Shorter Edition, p. 689

From the viewpoint of Christian belief, the essential inequality of all people is a central paradox, and it is the most painful one, of human experience. The paradox or "The Riddle of Inequality," as Paul Tillich calls it, is stated repeatedly in the Gospels: "For to him who has will more be given; and from him who has not, even what he has will be taken away" (Mark 4:25). Like other human mysteries, this riddle cannot be "solved" in the finite world. However, it must be a matter of faith to explore the implications of the riddle and to accept, finally and lovingly, the burden of living with(in) the riddle.

Tillich's sermon evidences this Christian approach to the riddle. In a very carefully directed analysis, Tillich investigates "the breadth and the depth of the riddle of inequality." He divides the investigation into three tightly organized sections: First, he explores what we have and whether or not we really have it; second, he raises the issue of inequality in original gifts (birth circumstances, etc.); third, he observes that some people use their talents and others don't. This leads him to the general human question "why has [some thing or other] *not* happened to me?" The final four paragraphs of the essay are devoted to positing a way of living with the unsolvable riddle. Tillich finds the "way," if not the specific solution, in belief in the unity of creation and the participation of the divine, as symbolically manifested in the cross, in that unity.

Analytical Considerations

1. What is the "riddle of inequality"?
2. Does Tillich solve the riddle? On the basis of what certainty? What is the "way" he proposes?
3. What is Tillich's purpose here?
4. Does the essence of Zen Buddhism, as set forth by Gilbert Highet in "The Mystery of Zen" (NR 1170, SE 705), offer a response to the riddle of inequality?
5. What textual clues indicate that this is a sermon?
6. Ask students to plot and evaluate the design of "The Riddle." Is Tillich's introduction effective? Analyze the elements of his opening paragraph. How has he divided the body of his essay? What techniques serve his purpose? What does Tillich do in the last four paragraphs?
7. How does Tillich use rhetorical questions in "The Riddle of Inequality"? Are they overused?
8. Ask students to ponder the significance of several key statements in this essay:
    a. "The growth of our lives is possible only because we have sacrificed the original gift of innocence. . . . No maturity is possible without this sacrifice."
    b. "In every revolution and in every war, the will to solve the riddle of inequality is a driving force. But neither war nor revolution can remove it."

c. "Each of us must consider the increase or the loss of what is given to him as a matter of his own responsibility."
d. "There is an ultimate unity of all beings, rooted in the divine life from which they come and to which they go. All beings, nonhuman as well as human, participate in it."
e. "In every death which we encounter, something of us dies; in every disease which we encounter, something of us tends to disintegrate."

9. How does Tillich weave the imagery as well as the content of the epigraph into his sermon?

Suggested Writing Assignments

1. Write an essay in response to Tillich's assertion "Those talents which are used, even with a risk of losing them, are those which we really have."

2. Write an essay in response to any of the excerpts in Analytical Consideration 8 above or to one of your own choice.

3. Write an essay comparing Tillich's definition of despair—"The inability of getting rid of oneself"—with Jean Paul Sartre's in "Existentialism" (NR 1193, SE 717). Are there responses to those issues consistently antithetical? Discuss the role of responsibility in the arguments put forth by Tillich and Sartre.

LANGSTON HUGHES

Salvation

The Norton Reader, p. 1139; Shorter Edition, p. 695

"Salvation" reveals in full measure Langston Hughes's gifts as a storyteller: economy and precision of language; a keen ear for dialogue; a sharp eye for descriptive detail; a detached ironic voice. Hughes's re-creation of a revival meeting set in rural America around 1914 or 1915 is a cultural document—an exposé of the sometimes dishonest theatrics of a manipulative preacher in front of a gullible flock of souls. It is also an account of an experience of considerable symbolic importance in Hughes's memory; as such it might be considered a rite of passage narrative.

Analytical Considerations

1. How is "Salvation" a study of several different personality types?

2. How do we know that "Salvation" was written by an adult? Why do students think that Hughes wrote it? Was it merely for autobiographical purposes?

3. What is the tone of Hughes's first sentence? Of his second sentence? What is the effect of paragraph 2, which consists of one four-word sentence?

4. Ask students to analyze Hughes's technique as a narrator. Is his narrative effective? Why or why not?

5. Compare/contrast Hughes's ability to recapture childhood experience with that of Dylan Thomas or Maya Angelou.

Suggested Writing Assignments

1. Write an essay on the ways in which "Salvation" re-creates a particular time and place. Do you think it is at all important that some characters are named but that no specific location is cited?

2. Write an essay on "Salvation" as a rite of passage narrative, discussing how Hughes's experience at the revival meeting changed his perception. Or write your own rite of passage narrative.

Additional questions on this essay will be found in the text (NR 1141, SE 697).

E. M. FORSTER

What I Believe

The Norton Reader, p. 1162; Shorter Edition, p. 697

Although E. M. Forster characterizes himself as someone possessing little faith, courage, or vision, much of his personal credo contradicts this rhetorical stance. Forster's chapter from *Two Cheers for Democracy* uses hypothetical situations to explain his deviance from traditional values ("if I had to choose between betraying my country and betraying my friend . . . ," for example).

Forster's "disbelief" becomes a matter of semantics since the reader is made aware of quite a few of his beliefs. The author would argue, however, that this is too strong a word for his tastes.

Analytical Considerations

1. Re: content
   a. How does Forster define "faith"?
   b. How does Forster favor democracy?
   c. How does Forster define "civilization"?
   d. What saves Forster from despair?
   e. Why does Forster distrust "Great Men"?

2. Suggest that students draw up a list of the values to which Forster subscribes; ask them to rank them in order of importance to him.

3. Ask students to consider "What I Believe" as a cultural document. Are there elements in the text that indicate that it is of a certain time and place? Is its relevance thus enhanced or diminished?

4. Is there a discrepancy between Forster's presentation of himself as a timid, insecure individual and what we learn of his personality from his writing style and freedom of expression? Compare these two "personalities."

5. You might lead students to assess how personal and idiosyncratic "What I Believe" is. One way to do that is to discuss rhetorical features like assumptions, generalizations, and evidence (or lack thereof). Forster's failure to supply evidence, whether from research or from testimony, seems to diminish the essay and certainly leaves him open to the charge of writing from an insulated position of privilege.

Suggested Writing Assignments

1. Write an essay in response to what may be Forster's most famous line: ". . . if I had to choose between betraying my country and betraying my friend, I hope I should have the guts to betray my country."

2. Write an essay articulating what you think would be Paul Tillich's response to Forster's "What I Believe."

3. Write an essay in response to this question: Has the passage of time ("What I Believe" is fifty years old) confirmed or denied Forster's judgments and predictions concerning history and religion?

GILBERT HIGHET

The Mystery of Zen

The Norton Reader, p. 1170; Shorter Edition, p. 705

In "The Mystery of Zen," Gilbert Highet, a distinguished teacher, writes about a German philosopher, Eugen Herrigel, who studied under a Zen master for six years. Highet is at least as concerned with the method by which Herrigel learned as with what he learned from his lengthy course in the art of Zen archery. At a deeper and somewhat more abstract level, the essay deals with the difficulties of describing the mystical dimension of human existence, which, Highet concludes, cannot be analyzed but must be lived to be understood.

Analytical Considerations

1. Re: content
   a. Who wrote *Zen and the Art of Archery*?

b. How long did Herrigel's lessons in Zen archery last?
c. What makes a shot in Zen archery "perfect"?
d. What does the word "Zen" mean?
e. What is the Buddha's most famous sermon called?

2. What is the "mystery of Zen"? Does Highet convey the mystery successfully?

3. What does "Zen meditation" mean to Highet? What techniques does he use to present his understanding?

4. Are students satisfied with the way Highet defines "meditation" in paragraph 15? Can it be "a way of life" in twentieth-century Western society?

5. How does Highet distinguish "philosophical teachers" from "mystical writers"?

6. Highet's discussion of mystical writers (paragraph 18) is worth considering, for he dwells upon the insufficiency of language "to describe experiences which are too abstruse for words." In what situations and in what ways does language fail us? Why do we "fall back on imagery and analogy"? Does this happen more often in poetry than prose? Why?

7. Do you accept Highet's assertion that "Zen is a religion rather than a philosophy"?

8. How do you know that Gilbert Highet appreciates and admires the Zen philosophy or practice?

Suggested Writing Assignments

1. Highet's charming, if self-indulgent, introduction to "The Mystery of Zen" suggests that one can get new meaning from books (or articles, or poems, or paintings, perhaps) that one returns to after some absence. Have you had any experience of this sort? Describe it in an essay.

2. Consider "The Mystery of Zen" as an essay on the art of teaching. Write an essay, "Zen and the Art of ____________," in which you detail the techniques of Zen instruction as they apply to an interest of yours.

Additional questions on this essay will be found in the text (NR 1178, SE 713).

VIRGINIA WOOLF

The Death of the Moth

The Norton Reader, p. 1179; Shorter Edition, p. 714

This essay, one of Virginia Woolf's best-known works of nonfiction prose, combines narrative and description in the service of definition. Woolf writes with feeling but not sentiment, offering her reader a carefully realized observation before speculating about the meaning of that observation.

Woolf plays the role of desultory observer and reporter in "The Death of the Moth." What begins as idle curiosity becomes conscious speculation, but no conclusions are drawn. Woolf's emotion is understated, and her prose is elegant rather than elegiac. Although she points to possible meaning immanent in the death throes of the moth, she does not overshadow the event itself with ponderous philosophical analysis.

Analytical Considerations

1. Ask students what aspects of "The Death of the Moth" stand out. Why? Imagery will likely be considered here. Have students select several images, and distinguish the primary appeal of each (visual, aural, tactile). Then ask them to determine how each image functions within the essay.
2. Does Woolf offer a thesis statement? Does she have a central point she wishes to make? Or is this a speculative exercise, more important for the writing than the content?
3. You might want students to describe the persona Woolf has created here. How does she create it? Is her use of the third person ("one") in much of the essay important in this regard? Why does she shift to the first person in the last paragraphs? Does she use language that creates a sense of emotional involvement or impact?
4. Compare Woolf's style in this selection to her style in "My Father: Leslie Stephen" (NR 146, SE 83).
5. How and to what effect has Woolf used a kind of triple focus (the world "out there"; the moth; the narrator) in this essay? What kind of context has she sought to create? Why?
6. What is the relationship between the life and death of the moth and the life and death of human beings in "The Death of the Moth"? Does Woolf offer any conclusions about death in this piece?

Suggested Writing Assignments

1. If the death of an animal has moved you to speculate on significant questions concerning existence, write an essay describing and analyzing the experience.
2. With ironic understatement, Woolf writes that "The insignificant little creature now knew death." Yet this little creature was not insignificant. Write an essay explaining that.

Additional questions on this essay will be found in the text (NR 1181, SE 716).

JEAN-PAUL SARTRE

Existentialism

The Norton Reader, p. 1193; Shorter Edition, p. 717

Existentialism is seemingly the most significant philosophy to be propounded in recent history, and this essay presents one of the most coherent statements we have of the existentialist position. Jean-Paul Sartre anchors his discussion to the famous existentialist catchphrase "existence precedes essence." What he does essentially, then, in the essay is develop the implications of this assertion. The phrase suggests, generally, that man is responsible for what he is and what he becomes. The existentialist position demands that one confront, and accept, the "anguish" concomitant with assuming responsibility for oneself and all mankind. It demands, according to Sartre, that one cope with the sense of "forlornness" that arises from the recognition that there is no higher authority than man and that there are no permanent values. It demands that one give up the illusion that one's fate is in other hands; in Sartre's terms, it demand that one "despair" of ultimate answers or consequences.

Sartre's essay, then, is clearly a position paper. But he does not wish merely to record the tenets of existentialism. His aim is also to convince the reader that existentialism as a philosophy is a more viable approach to life than traditional philosophies. At times, though he seems to be trying to justify some of the hard implications of his philosophy, Sartre is really pointing to the stature which existentialism attains through its bold refusal to deal with anything but intractable reality. He tries, finally, to show that since existentialism encourages one to say, "Think of the possibilities," or "Look what man has made and can make of himself," existentialism is an optimistic philosophy.

Analytical Considerations

1. Consider how effectively Sartre's various examples illustrate what he means by "forlornness," "anguish," and "despair." For instance, are the discussions of Abraham and the madwoman confusing, or do they clarify the concept of "anguish"?
2. Is the term "despair" ever clearly defined? Does the word describe or mean what Sartre says it does? Would a different word be more appropriate? Explain.
3. What does Sartre mean by his statement that "man is condemned to be free"?
4. Characterize Sartre's persona in this essay. Does the author come across as a logical and responsible thinker and writer?
5. Discuss the movement of ideas in the paragraph beginning

"Now for the existentialist." Does Sartre contradict himself within the paragraph. Explain.

Suggested Writing Assignments

1. Compare/contrast Sartre's "Existentialism" with Paul Tillich's "The Riddle of Inequality" (NR 1147, SE 689) as responses to the human situation in the modern world. Do the two share any values or attitudes?
2. As Sartre delineates it, do you find existentialism a viable approach to life or an appealing philosophy? If so, write an essay discussing its inherent values and the basis of its appeal.
3. Read E. M. Forster's "What I Believe" (NR 1162, SE 697). To what extent is Forster's philosophical position existentialistic? How would Sartre respond to Forster's creed?
4. Write an essay in response to Sartre's declaration that "Man is nothing else but what he makes of himself."

Additional questions on this essay will be found in the text (NR 1202, SE 726).

Index